# CAMDEN TOWN

## 4

## Klassenarbeitstrainer

Diesterweg
westermann

CAMDEN TOWN 4

Erarbeitet von
**Anna Maria Witty** und **Christine Götz**

Anna Maria Witty verbrachte vor und während ihres Studiums mehrere Jahre in Schweden, Spanien und in den USA. Seit einigen Jahren unterrichtet sie Englisch, Geschichte und Sozialkunde an Gymnasien und Fachoberschulen. Dabei sammelte sie Erfahrung im Erstellen von Materialien zum individuellen Lernen vor allem im Fach Englisch.

Christine Götz unterrichtet seit fast zwanzig Jahren Englisch, Deutsch und Geschichte an Gymnasien. Ein Schwerpunkt liegt dabei auf der Begleitung von individuellen Lernprozessen und auf der Betreuung von Referendaren und Referendarinnen. Sie hat bereits bei mehreren Lernhilfen zur Abiturvorbereitung in Englisch mitgewirkt.

westermann GRUPPE



Druck A⁴ / Jahr 2020
Alle Drucke der Serie A sind im Unterricht parallel verwendbar.

Redaktion: imprint, Zusmarshausen
Kontakt: lernhilfen@westermanngruppe.de
Layout: Druckreif! Sandra Grünberg, Braunschweig
Illustrationen: Hans-Jürgen Feldhaus, Münster
Umschlaggestaltung: blum DESIGN & KOMMUNIKATION, Hamburg und Druckreif! Sandra Grünberg, Braunschweig
Umschlagfoto: Dirk Schmidt/dsphotos.de
Druck und Bindung: Westermann Druck GmbH, Braunschweig

ISBN 978-3-425-**74123**-9

# Inhalt

# Inhalt

## Vorwort

Liebe Schülerin, lieber Schüler,

vor dir liegt der passende Klassenarbeitstrainer zu deinem Schulbuch
***Camden Town.***

Auf den ersten Seiten bekommst du Tipps zur Vorbereitung einer Klassenarbeit:

- Allgemeine Tipps
- Tipps zu Lernstrategien
- Spezielle Lerntipps zum Fach Englisch

Außerdem findest du hier einen Klassenarbeitsplaner, in den du eintragen kannst, wann du die nächste Klassenarbeit schreibst und was du bis dahin noch üben willst.

Die erfolgreiche Vorbereitung auf eine Klassenarbeit besteht aus drei Schritten: **Verstehen – Üben – Können.** Entsprechend ist auch dieser Klassenarbeitstrainer aufgebaut:

### Verstehen und Üben

Hinweiskästen ❗ erklären anhand von Beispielen noch einmal alle wichtigen Regeln und Begriffe. Lerntipps 💡 helfen dabei, sich die Regeln einzuprägen.
Direkt im Anschluss findest du abwechslungsreiche Aufgaben zum Üben des Lernstoffes. Solltest du bei der Bearbeitung einer Aufgabe einmal nicht weiterkommen, schau dir die Hinweiskästen und Lerntipps noch einmal genau an. Alle Übungen, zu denen es Audio-Dateien gibt, erkennst du an dem QR-Code und diesem Symbol 🎧. Scanne den Code mit einem Handy oder Tablet, dann gelangst du zu dem jeweiligen Hörtext. Alle Hörtexte sowie die Mitschriften dazu findest du auch im Internet unter **www.westermann.de/landing/camden-town.**

### Übungsklassenarbeiten

Wenn du genug geübt hast und dich sicher fühlst, kannst du als Test Übungsklassenarbeiten schreiben. Oben auf jeder Klassenarbeit ist das Kapitel aus deinem Schulbuch angegeben, auf das sich die Arbeit bezieht. Außerdem findest du dort eine Angabe, in welcher Zeit die Klassenarbeit bearbeitet werden soll. Achte darauf, dass du diese Zeit auch genau einhältst, denn nur so kannst du dich wirklich testen. Jede Aufgabe ist mit einer Punktzahl versehen. Anhand der Lösungen kannst du ermitteln, wie viele Punkte du erreicht hast und was du noch üben musst. Mithilfe der Smileys ☺ 😐 ☹ unter den Klassenarbeiten kannst du deinen Erfolg messen und erkennen, ob du noch weiter üben musst.
Die meisten Aufgaben kannst du direkt im Klassenarbeitstrainer lösen. Solltest du einmal nicht genug Platz finden, nimm einfach ein Heft zur Hand.

### Lösungsteil

Hinten im Klassenarbeitstrainer findest du die Lösungen zu allen Übungsaufgaben und Übungsklassenarbeiten. Du kannst die von dir bearbeiteten Aufgaben und Klassenarbeiten eigenständig kontrollieren oder jemand anderen bitten, es zu tun.

Wir wünschen dir viel Erfolg beim Üben für die nächste Klassenarbeit!

***Anna Maria Witty und Christine Götz***

# Lern-Hilfen zur Vorbereitung auf die Klassenarbeit

## 1. Allgemeine Lerntipps

Hier findest du Hinweise auf Lern- und Wiederholungstechniken, die du vielleicht schon kennengelernt, aber im Lauf der Zeit wieder vergessen hast – oder auch nie angewendet hast. Außerdem findest du hier Möglichkeiten, wie du immer selbstständiger mit der englischen Sprache umgehen kannst. Das wird zunehmend wichtig werden und ist nicht leicht zu üben. Verliere nicht die Geduld! Vor allem wenn du selbst Texte schreibst, wird es eine Weile dauern, bis du merkst, wie sehr du dich verbessert hast.

### Arbeitsmaterial

- Nach wie vor gilt: Führe deine Unterlagen sorgfältig und ordentlich. Achte darauf, dass du beim Abschreiben von Vokabeln oder Grammatikregeln keine Fehler einbaust, die du dann unter Umständen mitlernst!
- Halte in der Schule deine Materialien immer bereit! Das sollten sowohl dein Buch als auch deine Hefte und dein Schreibzeug sein. Dein Arbeitsplatz zu Hause sollte immer aufgeräumt und übersichtlich sein. Alles, was dich vom Lernen abhalten könnte, hat auf deinem Schreibtisch nichts verloren.

### Lernen von Vokabeln und Grammatik

Grundsätzlich gilt: Sorge dafür, dass du in Ruhe lernen kannst.
Wichtig ist, dass du immer wieder „ältere" Vokabeln und Grammatikregeln systematisch wiederholst. Dabei können dir folgende Tipps helfen:

- Mithilfe eines Karteikastens kannst du sehr einfach auch Vokabeln aus früheren Jahren wiederholen. Das ist allerdings vor allem dann sinnvoll, wenn du von Anfang an sorgfältig mit einem Karteikasten gearbeitet hast und die Vokabeln vollständig und fehlerfrei enthalten sind. Wenn dies nicht der Fall ist, macht das Neu-Anlegen eines Karteikastens einige Arbeit – es lohnt sich trotzdem.
- Eine andere Möglichkeit der Wiederholung ist, dass du die Vokabeln oder Grammatikregeln auf kleine Zettel schreibst und diese dann zu Hause aufhängst. Das kann beispielsweise der Badezimmerspiegel sein oder der Kühlschrank. So liest du die Vokabeln oder Grammatikregeln immer wieder (auch unbewusst) und du kannst sie dir leichter merken.
- Achte darauf, dass du dir nicht zu viel vornimmst! Stelle dir kleine Lern-Portionen zusammen, die du an einem Tag lernen willst. So kannst du ebenso die Vokabeln und die Grammatik aus den vergangenen Jahren systematischer, gezielter und übersichtlicher wiederholen. Dafür reichen 10 Minuten am Tag. Wenn du das wirklich (fast) jeden Tag machst, ist das sehr effektiv.
- Plane auch deine Lernpausen gut ein! Nach etwa 45 Minuten solltest du immer eine kurze(!) Pause einlegen, damit das Gelernte „sacken" kann, also im Gehirn verarbeitet wird.
- Nutze Eselsbrücken! Eine Merkhilfe sind außerdem Bilder zu einzelnen Vokabeln oder ganzen Wortfeldern, die du dir vorstellst oder in dein Vokabelheft dazumalst.
- Wenn du Vokabeln und Grammatik aufschreibst, dann versuche dabei, ganze Wortfelder von Anfang an systematisch und übersichtlich zu gestalten, indem du zu einem Wortfeld beispielsweise ein Cluster oder eine MindMap entwirfst – mit genügend Platz für spätere Ergänzungen.
- Wenn du das Gefühl hast, dass gar nichts geht, kann dir helfen, wenn du dir kleine Belohnungen überlegst. Wichtig ist, dass du dich dabei nicht selbst austrickst und du dir die Belohnung tatsächlich verdienst!
- Ganz wichtig ist nach wie vor, dass du in der Schule gut mitarbeitest. Das heißt nicht, dass du dich ständig melden musst – auch wenn das Sprechen natürlich vor allem im Unterricht geübt wird. Nimm dir also vor, dass du dich immer wieder

meldest. Vor allem solltest du aber aufmerksam sein und dem Lehrer gut zuhören. Denn sehr oft werden im Unterricht Dinge aus den vergangenen Jahren wiederholt. Zur Mitarbeit gehört, dass du dir das, was du im Unterricht gelernt hast, zu Hause gründlich noch einmal ansiehst. Und die Hausaufgaben solltest du grundsätzlich konzentriert und sorgfältig erledigen – das ist die beste Übung.

**Darüber hinaus gibt es noch viele weitere Möglichkeiten, wie du deine Englischkenntnisse üben und verbessern kannst.**

- Sieh dir deine Lieblingsfilme auf Englisch an. Meistens finden sich im Internet Ausschnitte oder Trailer für Filme, die dich interessieren. Wenn du Filme auf DVD ansiehst, kannst du die englische Version zunächst mit, später ohne Untertitel anschauen – so kannst du üben, Gesprochenes zu verstehen.
- Auch das Musikhören ist eine gute Übung. Versuche zunächst, deine (englischen) Lieblingslieder zu verstehen, ohne dass du die Texte nachschaust. Versuche dann zu erklären, worum es in dem Lied geht. Du musst nicht Wort für Wort übersetzen! Wenn du in einer Suchmaschine nach dem Text (Stichwort *lyrics* zusammen mit dem Titel des Lieds) suchst, wirst du feststellen, dass du vieles verstanden hast – vielleicht aber manches völlig falsch. Die englischen Lieder laut mitzusingen ist ebenfalls eine gute Sache.
- Bestimmt gibt es viele Themen, die dich interessieren. Warum nicht einfach einen Text zu einem Thema, das dich interessiert, auf Englisch lesen? Kürzere Texte zu allen möglichen Themen gibt es im Internet zum Beispiel im „Tea-Time Magazine" (teatime-mag.com), wo zudem schwierigere Wörter erklärt werden. Du kannst natürlich auch selbst nach englischsprachigen Blogs suchen. Außerdem gibt es regelmäßig erscheinende Zeitschriften mit Texten in vereinfachtem Englisch, die du ohne weiteres verstehst und in denen ebenfalls schwierige Wörter erklärt werden. Vielleicht gibt es ja bei dir an der Schule die Möglichkeit, eine solche Zeitschrift auszuleihen (z. B. „Spotlight").
- Und sicherlich gibt es viele Bücher, die du spannend, interessant oder lustig findest. Suche in der Bibliothek deiner Schule oder auch in der Bücherei deines Wohnortes! Auch neue und spannende Bücher, die du auf deutsch schon kennst oder gerne lesen würdest, kannst du oft schon auf Englisch verstehen, zum Beispiel „The Hunger Games" oder die „Harry-Potter"-Reihe.
- Im Internet gibt es eine ganze Reihe von kostenlosen Seiten für Englisch-Lerner. So werden zum Beispiel bei www.ego4u.de oder www.englisch-hilfen.de einfache Texte oder Übungen zu Grammatik und Vokabeln angeboten. Der Nachteil dieser Seiten liegt natürlich darin, dass sie sich nicht an Camden Town orientieren, sodass sich möglicherweise vieles findet, was für dich zu schwer oder unverständlich sein könnte.

## Sprechen und Schreiben

- Ansonsten kannst du natürlich das Formulieren selbst jederzeit üben, indem du im Alltag Leuten zuhörst. Stell dir dann vor, du bist ein Dolmetscher, der alles übersetzen soll. Merke dir die Wörter, die dir fehlen, und schlage sie zu Hause nach.
- Dein Englisch ist inzwischen sowieso gut genug, um es immer wieder „im Ernstfall" auszuprobieren. Wenn du zum Beispiel Touristen siehst, biete doch einfach deine Hilfe an, indem du fragst: *Can I help you?* Dann wirst du sehr schnell feststellen, wie gut du dich schon verständigen kannst.

## Freie Textproduktion

Je öfter du etwas selbst formulierst, desto besser wird dein Englisch im Lauf der Zeit werden. Schwierig dabei ist allerdings die Kontrolle der eigenen Texte. Du kannst

Freunde oder Klassenkameraden bitten, einen von dir verfassten Text durchzulesen, notfalls wird dein Lehrer zwischendurch einen kürzeren Text korrigieren.
Du selbst kannst deine eigenen Texte ebenfalls überprüfen – und das solltest du auf jeden Fall in Klassenarbeiten tun (und daher vorher geübt haben). Falls du das noch nicht gewohnt bist, kann dir die folgende Checkliste helfen. Sie bietet dir eine ganze Reihe von Leitfragen, mit denen du deinen Text Punkt für Punkt noch einmal durchlesen solltest.

- **Rechtschreibung**: Ist jedes Wort richtig geschrieben? (Betrachte dafür den Text Wort für Wort „von hinten", indem du mit einem Lineal oder Blatt den Text abdeckst und dann, mit dem letzten Wort beginnend, Wort für Wort aufdeckst, sodass du die einzelnen Wörter ohne ihren Zusammenhang liest.)
- **Satzbau**: Ist in jedem Satz die Reihenfolge Subjekt – Verb – Objekt eingehalten? Sind die Fragen richtig mit *do* oder einem Hilfsverb gebildet? Sind alle Verneinungen richtig mit *do* oder einem Hilfsverb gebildet? (Hier kannst du dir einfache Sätze als Muster merken, zum Beispiel für den Aussagesatz *I go to school*, für den Fragesatz *Do you go to school?* und für die Verneinung *He doesn't go to school.*) Sind alle anderen Angaben und Adverben an den passenden Stellen eingesetzt?
- **Zeiten**: Habe ich in jedem Satz die richtige Zeit verwendet? Habe ich alle Signalwörter gefunden? Habe ich die unregelmäßigen Verben richtig gebildet? Habe ich das Passiv richtig verwendet?
- **Adjektive/Adverben:** Habe ich bei den Wörtern, die sich auf eine Handlung oder ein Adjektiv beziehen, das Adverb verwendet? Habe ich die Steigerung mit *-er* oder mit *more* richtig angewandt?
- **Artikel**: Ist bei den bestimmten Artikeln immer klar, auf was sich der Artikel bezieht? Habe ich unbestimmte und bestimmte Artikel richtig verwendet?
- **Hilfsverben**: Habe ich die Hilfsverben sinnvoll eingesetzt? Habe ich an den nötigen Stellen die Ersatzformen richtig gewählt?
- **Präpositionen**: Habe ich die Präpositionen sinnvoll ausgewählt?
- **Relativsätze**: Habe ich bei Relativsätzen das richtige Relativpronomen (*which*? *who*? *that*?) ausgewählt? Habe ich, wo nötig, ein Komma gesetzt?
- **Satzverknüpfungen**: Habe ich die Sätze sinnvoll verknüpft?
- **Sprachebene**: Habe ich Sätze mit Nebensätzen verwendet?
- **Stil**: Habe ich passende und abwechslungsreiche Wörter gewählt?

Der Inhalt und die Form müssen je nach Aufgabenstellung überprüft werden. Leitfragen dazu findest du in den Übungsteilen dieses Buches bei den Aufgaben zur Textproduktion.

> Denke immer daran: Selbst wenn nicht jeder Text, den du schreibst, korrigiert wird, ergibt sich die Übung schon allein dadurch, dass du eigenständig formulierst und dir dadurch immer wieder ins Gedächtnis rufst, was dabei wichtig ist! Mithilfe dieser Checkliste kannst du nun überprüfen, welche Bereiche du schon richtig gut kannst und in welchen Bereichen kaum Verbesserungen nötig sind. Du siehst aber gleichzeitig, wo dein Englisch noch Schwächen zeigst. Merke dir diese Bereiche und überprüfe sie in den Klassenarbeiten ganz gezielt!

## 2. Tipps zur Vorbereitung auf die Klassenarbeit

- Nach der Klassenarbeit ist vor der Klassenarbeit: Die Vorbereitung auf eine Klassenarbeit beginnt immer unmittelbar nach der letzten Klassenarbeit.
- Mit der gezielten Vorbereitung solltest du etwa zwei Wochen vorher beginnen. Erstelle dir deinen persönlichen Trainingsplan mithilfe des Klassenarbeitsplaners in diesem Buch! Dein Lehrer wird dich rechtzeitig informieren, was genau geprüft

wird. Scheue dich nicht, nachzufragen, was du selbst wiederholen solltest, und ergänze eventuell den Trainingsplan.
- Denke immer daran, zur Klassenarbeit ausgeruht zu sein. Am Tag vor der Arbeit solltest du dir für deinen Trainingsplan nur noch kleine Wiederholungspäckchen vornehmen und frühzeitig zu Bett gehen.
- Halte in der Klassenarbeit deine Arbeitsmaterialien (Füller, Textmarker, Bleistift, Lineal etc.) bereit.
- Bewahre vor allem einen kühlen Kopf, auch wenn du vielleicht am Anfang ein wenig nervös bist. Verschaffe dir zunächst in aller Ruhe einen Überblick über das, was von dir erwartet wird. Teile dir, noch bevor du anfängst, die Zeit gut ein. Achte dabei darauf, dass du dir für die Aufgaben, die mehr Punkte einbringen, entsprechend mehr Zeit nimmst! Beginne mit den Aufgaben, die dir am leichtesten fallen, dann hast du mehr Zeit für die schwierigeren Aufgaben.
- Immer häufiger wirst du selbstständig ganze Texte verfassen müssen. Achte auch dabei ganz genau auf die Aufgabenstellung. Überlege dir gut, welche Art von Text (Brief, E-Mail, Zeitungsartikel etc.) verlangt wird und welche Inhalte enthalten sein sollten. Nimm dir für diese Aufgaben genügend Zeit. Wenn es doch knapp werden sollte, dann versuche trotzdem, etwas zu schreiben – wenn nichts auf dem Papier steht, kann von Vornherein nichts bewertet werden. Plane also so, dass du auf jeden Fall etwas schreiben kannst, und denke daran, einen kleinen Zeitpuffer zur Verfügung zu haben – du solltest am Schluss den Text noch einmal durchlesen und kleinere Fehler verbessern können!

## 3. Die Arbeit mit diesem Buch

- Dieser Klassenarbeitstrainer enthält zu jedem „Theme“ von Camden Town einen Übungs- und einen Aufgabenteil. Übrigens: In Bayern werden Klassenarbeiten Schulaufgaben genannt.
- Im Übungsteil finden sich immer Aufgaben zu den Vokabeln, die in deinem Textbuch fett gedruckt sind, sowie zu den einzelnen Grammatikkapiteln des „Theme“. Außerdem kannst du hier noch einmal Listening Comprehension, Reading Comprehension und die im „Theme“ vorgestellten Aufgaben zur Textproduktion üben. Zudem findest du Tipps zur Bearbeitung der jeweiligen Aufgabenformen.
- Im Aufgabenteil werden dir jeweils zwei Beispiel-Klassenarbeiten angeboten, die du in 45 Minuten bearbeiten kannst. Versuche, sie zunächst zu bearbeiten, ohne dass du in den Lösungen nachschlägst. Die meisten Aufgaben kannst du mithilfe des Lösungsteils selbst korrigieren und bewerten, sodass du erkennst, welche Aufgabenbereiche du noch einmal wiederholen solltest. Mache dann einfach nochmal Übungen aus dem Übungsteil, vergiss dabei nicht, in den Regeln nachzulesen.
- Etwas problematisch ist die Korrektur und Bewertung der Aufgaben zur Textproduktion. Für die Korrektur der Sprache kannst du die Checkliste aus diesem Vorwort zu Hilfe nehmen; im Lösungsteil findest du darüber hinaus Hinweise darauf, wie viele Punkte du dir für Sprache, Inhalt und Form geben kannst.

**Gebrauchsanweisung für den Klassenarbeitsplaner:** Der Planer soll dich bei einer vernünftigen Lernplanung unterstützen. Ausgehend vom Stoff, der in der Klassenarbeit behandelt werden wird, teilst du das Arbeitspensum zeitlich ein. Frage ggf. bei deiner Lehrkraft nach! Ein wichtiger Zwischenschritt ist, nach einigen Tagen der Vorbereitung zu erkennen, wo du noch Schwächen hast. Darauf solltest du dich besonders stürzen. Aber vergiss nicht, dich für deine Arbeit zu belohnen (Kino, gemeinsamer Fernsehabend, Sport ...).

## Mein Klassenarbeitsplaner

| | Beispiel | Klassenarbeit 1<br>Termin: | Klassenarbeit 2<br>Termin: |
|---|---|---|---|
| Thema der Klassenarbeit | Du kannst bei deiner Lehrerin oder deinem Lehrer erfragen, was alles drankommt. | | |
| 14 bis 10 Tage vor der Klassenarbeit | Wichtig ist es, rechtzeitig zu beginnen: Trage hier ein, welche Aufgaben aus dem Klassenarbeitstrainer für die kommende Arbeit wichtig sind (z. B. Seiten 13 – 18, Aufgaben 4 – 8). Versuche, etwa die Hälfte der Übungen zu schaffen. | erledigt: ☐ | erledigt: ☐ |
| 9 bis 6 Tage vor der Klassenarbeit | Mache jetzt alle Aufgaben, die du die Tage vorher noch nicht geschafft hast, und wiederhole alle, die du sehr schwer fandest. Bearbeite dann eine der Klassenarbeiten in „deinem“ Kapitel. | erledigt: ☐ | erledigt: ☐ |
| erkannte Schwächen | Vielleicht hast du beim Abgleich mit den Lösungen erkannt, wo du noch Schwächen hast. Gib diese hier in Stichpunkten an (z.B. *connectives)*. | erledigt: ☐ | erledigt: ☐ |
| 5 bis 3 Tage vor der Klassenarbeit | Suche die Erklärungen zu den Themen, die dir Schwierigkeiten machen, und übe vor allem dazu. Bearbeite die zweite Klassenarbeit des Kapitels. | erledigt: ☐ | erledigt: ☐ |
| Zwischen-belohnung | Vergiss nicht, dich für deine Arbeit zu belohnen; vielleicht gehst du mit Freunden ins Kino … | | |
| die letzen beiden Tage vor der Klassenarbeit | Stürze dich darauf, was dir bei der zweiten Probeklassenarbeit schwer fiel. Wiederhole auch einige einfache Aufgaben, das beruhigt und hilft dagegen, etwas zu vergessen, was du schon konntest. | erledigt: ☐ | erledigt: ☐ |

| | Klassenarbeit 3<br><br>Termin: | Klassenarbeit 4<br><br>Termin: | Klassenarbeit 5<br><br>Termin: |
|---|---|---|---|
| Thema der Klassenarbeit | | | |
| 14 bis 10 Tage vor der Klassenarbeit | erledigt: ☐ | erledigt: ☐ | erledigt: ☐ |
| 9 bis 6 Tage vor der Klassenarbeit | erledigt: ☐ | erledigt: ☐ | erledigt: ☐ |
| erkannte Schwächen | erledigt: ☐ | erledigt: ☐ | erledigt: ☐ |
| 5 bis 3 Tage vor der Klassenarbeit | erledigt: ☐ | erledigt: ☐ | erledigt: ☐ |
| Zwischen-belohnung | | | |
| die letzen beiden Tage vor der Klassenarbeit | erledigt: ☐ | erledigt: ☐ | erledigt: ☐ |

## Working with words

### 1 School rules

Fill in the missing words. Some hints are given in brackets.

The rules at Lake Park are very strict: The use of (1)____________ (2)____________ is (3)____________: cell phones must be put (4) ____________ and can be used only in an emergency. Gambling is strictly (5) ____________ (= forbidden). (6) ____________ like chewing gum paper must be (7) ____________ properly. Students must have their (8) ____________ with them at all times. Students must wear (9) ____________ (= angemessen) (10) ____________ (= trousers, skirts etc) in the (11) ____________ (= corridors) and in the (12) ____________ (13) ____________ outside the building. Students mustn't use (14) ____________ words or (15) ____________ anybody. No (16) ____________ (17) ____________ (= anstößiges Benehmen) will be tolerated.

### 2 German – English

Find the English words. Use the parts of the words given in the box.

> **ack • ad • ad • ag • ate • bi • chase • ci • cri • dis • ex • fer • ger • help • ledge • li • now • one • other • pur • re • self • si • sing • spon • suf • tage • ti • ti • ty • van • ver • wise • ze**

ertragen – ____________

Werbung, Reklame – ____________

ansonsten – ____________

Nachteil – ____________

sich (an etwas) bedienen – ____________

zugeben, anerkennen – ____________

kritisieren – ____________

übertreiben – ____________

käuflich erwerben – ____________

Verantwortung – ____________

### 3 Expressing your opinion

Answer to the following statements. Start your sentences with a phrase expressing the German words.

1. "I think it's awful that we can't use our cell phones at school." – (Was mich betrifft ...)

____________________________________________

____________________________________________

2. "I don't like apple pie!" – (Ich persönlich glaube ...)

________________________________________________

3. "Chicago is a very dirty city." – (Ich muss zugeben, dass ...)

________________________________________________

4. "Schools in Germany are very good." – (Ich würde sagen, dass ...)

________________________________________________

## Grammar: mixed tenses and more

Im Englischen ist genau geregelt, wann welche Zeitform verwendet wird.
Hier findest du noch einmal einen Überblick über die Formen, die dir bereits bekannt sind, und die wichtigsten Regeln für ihre Anwendung. Diese Grundlagen müssen dir unbedingt bekannt sein!

• *see also TB p. 162–164*

!

***Simple present***
Es wird verwendet für eine (wiederholte) Handlung in der Gegenwart, für allgemein gültige Aussagen und für aufeinander folgende Handlungen.
**Bildung:** Form des Infinitivs, *-s* bei *he/she/it*
**Aussage:** *She goes to the cinema.*
**Verneinung:** *She doesn't go to the cinema.*
**Frage:** *Does she go to the cinema?*
**Aussage im Passiv:** *The letter is written by John.*
**Signalwörter:** *always, usually, normally, often, sometimes, every (Sunday) ...*

***Present progressive***
Es wird verwendet für eine Handlung, die gerade abläuft.
**Bildung:** Präsens von *be* + *ing*-Form des Verbs
**Aussage:** *He is playing football.*
**Verneinung:** *He isn't playing football.*
**Frage:** *Is he playing football?*
**Aussage im Passiv:** *The letter is being written by John right now.*
**Signalwörter:** *at the moment, just now, right now ...*

***Simple past***
Es wird verwendet für eine (wiederholte) Handlung in der Vergangenheit und für aufeinander folgende Handlungen in der Vergangenheit.
**Bildung:** Verb + *-ed* bzw. *past*-Form der unregelmäßigen Verben
**Aussage:** *They went to the cinema. They watched the movie.*
**Verneinung:** *They didn't go to the cinema. They didn't watch the movie.*
**Frage:** *Did they go to the cinema? Did they watch the movie?*
**Aussage im Passiv:** *The movie was watched by everybody.*
**Signalwörter:** *yesterday, two days ago, in 1990, last Friday ...*

### *Past progressive*
Es wird verwendet für eine Handlung, die in der Vergangenheit ablief, vor allem, wenn diese durch eine andere Handlung unterbrochen wurde. Betont wird der Ablauf der Handlung.
**Bildung:** *was/were + ing*-Form des Verbs
**Aussage:** *While she was baking a cake, the doorbell rang.*
**Verneinung:** *She wasn't baking a cake when the doorbell rang.*
**Frage:** *Was she baking a cake when the doorbell rang?*
**Aussage im Passiv:** *The letter was being written when the boss called.*
**Signalwörter:** *when, while*

### *Present perfect simple*
Es wird verwendet für eine Handlung, die bis in die Gegenwart andauert (oder deren Ergebnis noch eine Rolle spielt), für eine eben abgeschlossene Handlung und für eine Handlung, die bis zum Zeitpunkt der Äußerung noch nie stattgefunden hat.
*Bildung: have/has + -ed* bzw. *past-participle*-Form der unregelmäßigen Verben
**Aussage:** *John has written the letter.*
**Verneinung:** *John hasn't written the letter yet.*
**Frage:** *Has John written the letter?*
**Aussage im Passiv:** *The letter hasn't been written yet.*

### *Past perfect simple*
Es wird verwendet für eine Handlung, die vor einem bestimmten Zeitpunkt in der Vergangenheit stattgefunden hat.
**Bildung:** *had + -ed* bzw. *past-participle*-Form der unregelmäßigen Verben
**Aussage:** *John went home. His wife had called.*
**Verneinung:** *John didn't go home. His wife hadn't called.*
**Frage:** *John went home. Had his wife called?*
**Aussage im Passiv:** *John sent the letter. He had written it in his lunch break.*
**Signalwörter:** *yet* (+ Zeitpunkt in der Vergangenheit), *until that day ...*

### *Will-future*
Es wird verwendet für ein Geschehen in der Zukunft, das nicht beeinflussbar ist, für einen spontanen Entschluss und für Vorhersagen, die auf Vermutungen beruhen.
**Bildung:** *will* + Verb
**Aussage:** *The students will pass the test.*
**Verneinung:** *The students won't (= will not) pass the test.*
**Frage:** *Will the students pass the test?*
**Aussage im Passiv:** *The test will be passed by everybody.*

### *Going-to-future*
Es wird verwendet für eine Handlung, die in der Zukunft beabsichtigt und geplant ist, und für Vorhersagen, die auf logischen Schlussfolgerungen beruhen.
**Bildung:** *is/are + going to* + Verb
**Aussage:** *Karl is going to spend one year in the USA.*
**Verneinung:** *Karl isn't going to spend one year in the USA.*
**Frage:** *Is Karl going to spend one year in the USA?*
**Aussage im Passiv:** *The school team is going to be celebrated.*

## 4 Karl's first week

After his first week in Chicago Karl talked to his host sister Laura.
Fill in the correct forms of the verbs.

**Laura**: So how (1) ______________________ (you – like) your first days here?

**Karl**: It (2) ______________________ (be) a great time so far! I (3) ______________________ (meet) some boys at school yesterday, and they (4) ______________________ (invite) me to a party at the weekend. I (5) ______________________ (not – go – usually) to parties very often, but I (6) ______________________ (go) to this party!

**Laura**: That's great! I'm sure you (7) ______________________ (have) a lot of fun! Where is it?

**Karl**: It's not far from the school building at Kevin's house.

**Laura**: Oh, I know that place! Kevin's parties are the best. I (8) ______________________ (go) to one of them last year. I (9) ______________________ (buy) a new dress, but while I (10) ______________________ (dance), somebody (11) ______________________ (spill = *verschütten*) his drink over it, so I (12) ______________________ (must – throw) it away. But the party was worth it!

**Karl**: That sounds fine! (13) ________________________________ (you – come), too?

Laura: Well, I (14) ______________________ (not – invite/passive!) yet. I (15) ______________________ (call) Kevin later. I know he (16) ______________________ (take part) in a meeting of the school magazine group right now, so he won't be home at the moment.

## 5 Present perfect and simple past

Cross out the wrong form.

***Present perfect*** – Die Handlung spielt in der Gegenwart noch eine Rolle.
*She has broken her leg.* = Sie trägt immer noch einen Gips am Bein.

***Simple past*** – Die Handlung ist abgeschlossen.
*She broke her leg.* = Sie ist (jetzt) wieder völlig gesund.

1. Everybody **has brought / brought** something to eat, so there is enough for everybody at the party.
2. Yesterday Kevin **has bought / bought** a huge cake, too, but his dog **has eaten/ate** half of it.
3. Karl **has put / put** on his best jeans. Now he feels like a movie star at the party.
4. He **has wanted / wanted** to wear his new shirt, too, but it is dirty and he **hasn't washed / didn't wash** it yet.
5. Laura **has been invited / was invited**, too, and now she is very happy to join the party.
6. She **has even bought / even bought** a new dress again, although last year her dress **has been completely ruined / was completely ruined**!

**!**

Das *present perfect progressive* wird verwendet für eine Handlung, die bis in die Gegenwart andauert, wobei nicht das Ergebnis betont wird, sondern die andauernde Handlung selbst.
Deshalb sind all jene Zeitangaben, die betonen, **wie lange** schon etwas dauert, Signalwörter.

Nicht vergessen: Bei der Angabe eines **Zeitpunkts** wird *since* verwendet (... *since 2010*), bei der Angabe eines **Zeitraums** wird *for* verwendet (... *for two years*).

## 6 Present perfect progressive

Talk about Karl's new friends at Lake Park.

1. Marvin – play football – three years • 2. Patrick – work for the school magazine – 2013
3. Maureen – dance in the cheerleader group – 2012 • 4. Karen – act – (only) six months

1. Marvin is a great quarterback. ______________________________

2. Patrick always interviews the new teachers. ______________________________

3. Maureen is going to attend a dance academy after school. ______________________________

______________________________

4. Karen can't take the role of Juliet. ______________________________

## 7 be supposed to/ be expected to

Fill in the missing words. Use *be expected to*, *be supposed to*, *must*, *mustn't* or *needn't*.
It's the Wednesday of the homecoming week at Lake Park High School – it's the Homecoming T-shirt Day!

Die Formulierungen *be supposed to* und *be expected to* geben an, was man tun sollte bzw. was von einem erwartet wird. Eine stärkere Erwartung wird mit dem Hilfsverb *should* ausgedrückt.
Die stärkste Erwartungshaltung wird mit den Hilfsverben *must* (= müssen) bzw. *mustn't* (= nicht dürfen) ausgedrückt.

1. The students ____________________ buy their own t-shirts in the cafeteria.

2. But they ____________________ buy a t-shirt which is too tight and therefore inappropriate.

3. They ____________________ wear the t-shirt for the Powder Puff game in the evening, too.

4. But they ____________________ wear the t-shirt if it is dirty.

5. They____________________ carry their ID card even if they wear the t-shirt.

*Connectives* – Mithilfe von **Verknüpfungen** können Gedankengänge strukturiert und Texte zusammenhängend gestaltet werden. Wichtig ist, dass die logischen Verbindungen stimmig sind.
Vor allem zwei grammatikalische Möglichkeiten bieten sich an: Konjunktionen stellen eine logische Verbindung her, indem sie einen Nebensatz einleiten. Adverben stellen eine logische Verbindung her, indem sie als Ergänzung in einem Satz verwendet werden.
Häufig vorkommende Sinnrichtungen von *connectives* sind:
zeitliche Angaben (z. B. *as soon as, after, meanwhile …*)
Angaben zu Grund oder Folge (z. B. *because, so, due to, thanks to …*)
Gegenüberstellungen (z. B. *although, nevertheless, on the one hand – on the other hand, even though …*)

Im Textbook auf S. 154 findest du eine Übersicht über einige weitere wichtige *connectives*.

## 8 Connectives

Choose one of the connectives to link the two sentences. Underline the correct connective.

1. The Powder Puff football game was a great success for Lake Park High School. Their team won 79–35. (although / because)
2. Patton High School was defeated. They had scored 12 points in the first minutes. (although / meanwhile)
3. Lake Park's Lancers had great support. Their fans were fantastic. (due to / as soon as)
4. Debby Mayers scored 24 points. She was the best player. (thanks to / so)
5. The Susan G. Komen Breast Cancer Foundation is supported by Lake Park High School. They will get the money from the match. (thanks to / nevertheless)

# Reading/Listening

## 9 Chicago – the Windy City

Read the text carefully, then decide if the sentences are right or wrong.

*Bei einer Reading-Comprehension-Aufgabe kommt es darauf an, den Sinn des Textes zu verstehen. Dabei gibt es zwei Möglichkeiten: Entweder wird nach einzelnen Stellen gefragt oder nach dem Sinn eines ganzen Abschnitts. Lies dir deshalb die Aufgaben kurz durch, bevor du den Text liest!*
*Überfliege dann den Text und versuche, zu verstehen, was das Thema und was die Kernaussage jedes Abschnitts ist. Dazu musst du nicht jedes einzelne Wort kennen. Je nach Art der Aufgaben kannst du so gleich (am besten in verschiedenen Farben) markieren, welche Stellen sich auf welche Frage beziehen. Lies dann den Text gründlich und markiere die entscheidenden Stellen. Bearbeite danach die Aufgaben und lies (je nach Arbeitszeit) den Text noch einmal durch.*

**Chicago – the Windy City**
The first thing that you see when you come to Chicago is its nickname – Windy City. You will find it on t-shirts, on tea cups, on posters, on bags. It's everywhere!
But does the name really mean that Chicago is the windiest city in the world? By no means!
It's true, Chicago is located near Lake Michigan, one of the Great Lakes in the north of the USA. Because of this location, there are always strong winds which blow through the streets and through the high buildings. And these winds can be really chilling! But this is not the reason for the name. The name doesn't come from the "real" winds, but from the "winds" which are caused by the politicians, and the term is already more than 100 years old. At the end of the 19th century the USA wanted to celebrate the four hundredth anniversary of the discovery by Columbus, and people decided that they wanted a big show. Many cities wanted to be the place for the show – cities like New York or Washington, and of course Chicago. The political leaders in Chicago spoke a lot and promised a lot – and due to this the newspapers soon called Chicago the "windy city", thanks to the hot air that the politicians produced. So the name is not really a friendly one! For the 1893 World's Columbian Exposition in honor of Columbus it didn't matter – Chicago won the race and held the show.
It was also thanks to this show that Chicago still has a wonderful view of the lake. For the show the "White City" was built with many beautiful houses and funfairs and even a huge ferris wheel. After the show these buildings were destroyed again, most of them in a great fire in 1894. But the parks and areas were left, and people in Chicago have left them like that since then. And this is the reason why you have a wonderful view of the skyline if you take a Wendella boat for a river and lake trip!

| | | true | false |
|---|---|---|---|
| 1. | T-shirts with “Windy City” on them are popular souvenirs | ● | ● |
| 2. | Chicago is the windiest city in the world. | ● | ● |
| 3. | The wind can be very cold in Chicago. | ● | ● |
| 4. | The nickname comes from Chicago’s location near Lake Michigan. | ● | ● |
| 5. | The nickname “Windy City” was first used in the 1880s. | ● | ● |
| 6. | The nickname “Windy City” was used by politicians. | ● | ● |
| 7. | People in other cities thought that in Chicago people talk a lot of nonsense. | ● | ● |
| 8. | Columbus discovered America in 1593. | ● | ● |
| 9. | Chicago won the race for the show against New York. | ● | ● |
| 10. | The “White City” can still be seen today. | ● | ● |
| 11. | The “White City” was like a huge funfair – including a ferris wheel. | ● | ● |
| 12. | Wendella boats will bring you to the skyline. | ● | ● |

## 10 Cheerleaders

Read the instructions carefully, then listen to the text twice.
Then work on the assignments below.

*Beim Hörverstehen ist es wichtig, dass du noch vor dem Hören die Aufgaben gut durchgelesen hast. Dann erfährst du schon etwas zum Thema, zu den Sprechern, zur Situation etc. Überlege dir, auf welche Wörter du besonders hören solltest! Beim ersten Hören kannst du dann gleich (eventuell mit Bleistift) die Aufgaben ausfüllen. Achte dabei darauf, dass du weiter auf den Text hörst! Im Anschluss an das erste Hören erledigst du die Aufgaben, bei denen du die Lösung sicher weißt. Erst nach dem zweiten Hören kannst du dann die Aufgaben fertig bearbeiten. Schreibe jetzt mit Füller oder Kugelschreiber, radiere die Bleistiftnotizen nicht weg – das kostet zuviel Zeit!*

Fill in the missing words. Sometimes you can use the words from the text, sometimes you must find your own words.

1. Betty has been dancing for ______________________ years and wants to join the cheerleader team.
2. Nancy, the captain, ______________________ her to their next meeting.
3. Betty tells Nancy about the ______________________ which many Germans have about the cheerleaders.
4. Most Germans know about cheerleaders only from ______________________________________.
5. German people think that cheerleaders are ______________________, but this is not true – they are often very clever.
6. They also think that cheerleaders are ______________________, but that is wrong, too. They are often very friendly and nice.
7. And it’s not true that cheerleaders have to be ______________________ – but they must be good at dancing!

## Text production

Bei der **Mediation** (v. a. Deutsch–Englisch) kommt es darauf an, dass du die Aufgabenstellung genau beachtest. Es wird erwartet, dass du aus dem deutschen Material die jeweils passenden Informationen entnimmst (und das Überflüssige weglässt). Diese Informationen müssen je nach Aufgabenstellung in unterschiedlicher Weise wiedergegeben werden – du musst also auch die Regeln für die jeweilige Form beachten (z. B. E-Mail, Lexikonartikel etc.).

### 11 Rules

Mrs Harrington has asked Karl to write him an email about the most important rules at his school in Germany. Read the rules and write Karl's email (about 150 words). Use your exercise book.

**Hausordnung**

§ 1 Alle Schüler sind verpflichtet, pünktlich zum Unterricht zu erscheinen und die Materialien ordentlich und zuverlässig dabei zu haben.

§ 2 Der Unterricht beginnt um 8:00 Uhr und endet um 13:00 Uhr.

§ 3 Hausaufgaben sind grundsätzlich zu Hause anzufertigen.

§ 4 Der Gebrauch von Handys und Smartphones ist an der Schule grundsätzlich nicht erlaubt. Elektronische Geräte müssen deshalb ausgeschaltet in der Tasche aufbewahrt werden.

§ 5 Müll wird ordentlich getrennt und entsorgt. Der Hausmeister kontrolliert, ob dies immer gemacht wird.

§ 6 Es gibt keine Schuluniform. Die Kleidung muss jedoch stets angemessen sein. T-Shirts mit dem Schullogo können über die SMV gekauft werden.

Um deine eigene Arbeit zu kontrollieren, solltest du dir folgende Fragen stellen:

- Habe ich die Form der E-Mail richtig angewandt? (Siehe Aufgabe 14)
- Habe ich wirklich die Informationen ausgewählt, die für die Schulleiterin interessant sind?
- Habe ich einen passenden Ton verwendet?
- Ist der Text sprachlich richtig verfasst?

Gehe dazu auch die Leitfragen im Vorwort (S. 8) durch.

### 12 Personal statement

Karl wants to join Lake Park's soccer team. So he has to write a personal statement to the coach. Write that statement (about 150 words). Explain why you want to join the team, why you chose soccer and why the team would profit.
Use your exercise book.

Um deine eigene Arbeit zu kontrollieren, solltest du dir folgende Fragen stellen:

- Habe ich erklärt, warum ich dem Team beitreten will, warum ich Fußball spielen will und welche Vorteile mein Beitritt für die Mannschaft hat?
- Habe ich den Text entsprechend in Abschnitte gegliedert?
- Habe ich die Form mit Anrede und Unterschrift eingehalten?
- Habe ich den richtigen Ton getroffen – neutral und höflich?
- Habe ich ganz konkret meine Stärken, Ansichten und Erwartungen benannt, ohne dass ich allgemeine Aussagen wiedergegeben habe?
- Ist das Statement sprachlich richtig verfasst?

Gehe dazu auch die Leitfragen im Vorwort (S. 8) durch.

## 13 Article for the school magazine

Write a short article for the Lake Park High School magazine about "Texas Tuesday" (about 150 words). Use the information given below and add your own ideas if necessary.
Use your exercise book. You will find some tipps on the following page.

*I really love this day. It's a good opportunity to see the students and teachers from a different point of view. (Mr Miller, teacher)*

*It's great fun to see all the teachers in their cowboy hats! (Karen, student)*

Texas Tuesday

*I have to admit that the students seem to enjoy this day. Personally, I think that days like this are nonsense. We have more important things to do at school. (Mrs Harrington, guidance counselor)*

Ein Artikel für die Schülerzeitung muss nicht lang, sollte aber spannend und lebendig sein!
Stelle dir also folgende Fragen:
- Habe ich eine packende, knackige Überschrift gefunden?
- Habe ich den Text in Absätze eingeteilt?
- Werden im ersten Absatz die Fragen *Wer?*, *Was?*, *Wann?*, *Wo?* und *Warum?* beantwortet?
- Habe ich mit abwechslungsreichen Adjektiven und Zitaten den Text lebendig gestaltet?
- Habe ich persönliche Eindrücke oder Ansichten einbezogen?
- Habe ich die vorhandenen Informationen verwendet und mit eigenen Ideen ergänzt?
- Ist der Artikel sprachlich richtig verfasst?

Gehe dazu auch die Leitfragen im Vorwort (S. 8) durch.

## 14 Email

Mr McSweeny has asked Karl to write him an email about his first days at Lake Park High School. He wants to know ...
- about his first impressions of the sports program at Lake Park,
- if Karl wants to join one of the teams and
- what he likes most about the city of Chicago.

Write Karl's email (about 150 words).
Use your exercise book.

Bei einer E-Mail gibt es Vorgaben, die immer eingehalten werden müssen.
Stelle dir deshalb folgende Leitfragen:
- Habe ich den Empfänger/den Betreff genannt?
- Habe ich eine passende Anrede verwendet? (z. B. *Dear Sir or Madam, Dear Mrs Harrington* ...)
- Habe ich im ersten Abschnitt den Anlass für mein Schreiben genannt?
- Habe ich im ganzen E-Mail immer wieder den Adressaten im Blick, indem ich Bezug auf den bisherigen Kontakt nehme (*You've told me that* ...) oder Fragen stelle?
- Habe ich eine passende Schlussformel (*Best regards, Yours sincerely* ...) gefunden?
- Habe ich meinen eigenen Namen am Ende des E-Mails ergänzt?
- Habe ich einen für den Adressaten passenden Ton getroffen?
- Ist die E-Mail sprachlich richtig verfasst?

Gehe dazu auch die Leitfragen im Vorwort (S. 8) durch.

Zeit: 45 min Beginn ______ Ende ______

## At Lake Park High School – Test 1

### 1 Listening comprehension: school spirit

I. Listen to "School spirit".
There is something wrong in these statements. Write down the correct sentences.
Use your exercise book.

1. In the USA students go to school to learn.
2. At American high schools, sport is something very unpopular.
3. In the USA, young people do sports mostly in clubs or other associations.
4. In the USA, school lessons usually start at 9 o'clock.
5. All teams have training sessions for two or three hours a week.

Complete the sentences.

6. School teams are for example football, ______________________, ______________________ or ______________________.
7. Before you can join a team, you must take part in the ______________________ .
8. You can be a member of different teams, because every sport is done ______________________.

___ / 5

II. Fill in the missing words.

Football is the most important and ______________________ sport at high schools. The players always have a lot of fans, but they must suffer ______________________ times, too. All students and parents ______________________ their teams. They put up posters in the school ______________________ or paint the windows of ______________________ , for example.

___ / 5

III. Tick off the correct sentences.

- The parents don't care much about the teams.
- The parents are very interested in their children's teams.
- The parents drive very long ways to watch the matches.
- The parents often can't watch the matches because they have to work.
- The students are often less excited than their parents.
- The parents often have to calm down the students.
- The schools always pay a lot of money for their teams.
- The schools can't pay their teams much money.
- Each player needs at least $400 for one season.
- A football player needs at least three different outfits.
- The parents must pay a lot of money for the outfits, especially for cheerleaders.
- Sports is more expensive in small towns.

___ / 5

## 2 Vocabulary: Mrs Harrington

Fill in the missing words.

This is what Mrs Harrington thought when she arrived one morning at Lake Park High School:

"Thank God – no teacher is ill today! So everybody of the ____________________ will be here. And the buses are not late either – it's good that Lake Park is ____________________ so near Chicago. Oh, there are some students outside! What do they want now? They all ____________________ (= go to) different classes. Maybe Henry has got a question. He is only in his first year – he's a ____________________ . And I'm sure Jack just wants to ask if he has ____________________ high scores to get a scholarship. And Linda – why is she here again? I know that she wants to work in a hospital. I have already talked to her about becoming a ____________________ . Ah, and there's this new German student, Karl. Maybe he wants to become a member of the marching band – maybe he wants to ____________________ the marching band? In which year at high school is he? Which ____________________ is he in?

8

## 3 Grammar: simple past/present perfect

Fill in the verb in the simple past or in the present perfect.

When Laura comes home from school in the evening, she talks to her mother about her day:

"Mr Miller was angry, because he can't find my homework, but I'm sure I ____________________ (give) it to him yesterday! I ____________________ (meet) Jane just now. She's a really good friend! Kevin ____________________ (invite) me to his party on Friday. Can I go there? Please? ____________________ (you – see) Karl? He must be here now! Last week Karl ____________________ (talk) to me about his school in Germany. It must be very small – there are only 600 students! I ____________________ (never – see) a school like that here in the USA!

6

## 4 Grammar: present perfect progressive

Fill in the verb in the present perfect simple or the present perfect progressive.

Mrs Pulaski usually starts the day by telling her family what to do and what to remember:

"John, drink your cup of coffee now. It ______________________ (stand) around for half an hour, so it must be cold now! – Nick, your teacher told me that you must bring your book today. ______________________ (you – pack – already) it into your bag? – Laura, don't be nervous about your English test. You ______________________ (learn) for two hours yesterday, so I'm sure you know everything! – Nick, you needn't buy a new t-shirt. Your old one is clean again. But be careful with it now – I ______________________ (work) on it for hours yesterday! – Karl, ______________________ (you – tell) Mrs Harrington that you would like to join the soccer team already? – I'm sure they will let you join the team. You ______________________ (play) soccer for years in Germany!"

6

## 5 Grammar: mixed tenses

Fill in the verbs in the correct tense.

Debby Mayers is Lake Park's team captain. After the Powder Puff game the girls were very happy.

**Debby**: We have played really well! What a success!

**Karen**: (1) ____________________ (you – see) how all the people supported us? When Maizie scored the final goal, everybody (2) ____________________ (stand) in their seats!

**Maizie**: Yeah! But they didn't only cheer for me – you (3) ____________________ (pass) me the ball before.

**Debby**: You see – we are a good team! Hey, (4) ____________________ (anybody – see) my t-shirt? I (5) ____________________ (look) for it for half an hour now, but I can't find it.

**Karen**: I (6) ____________________ (pack) my bag right now. Maybe it's under it. Here it is!

**Debby**: Thank you. And now who (7) ____________________ (go) to Kevin's party? He (8) ____________________ (invite) the whole team. If we (9) ____________________ (win) again next year, I (10) ____________________ (give) a party myself!

10

## 6 Text production: newspaper article (mediation)

Karl has told Laura that at his school in Germany there is a soccer match between teachers and students every year. Now Laura has asked him to write an article for the Lake Park High School magazine about that.
Write the article (about 150 words). Use the information given below and add your own ideas if necessary. Use your exercise book.

**Ergebnisliste der Spiele Lehrer gegen Schüler**
2011: 5:7 – 2012: 6:7 – 2013: 1:4 – 2014: 4:7 – 2015: 3:4

**Text von der Schul-Homepage**
*Die etwas andere Begegnung*

Bereits zu Schulbeginn sah man die ersten Grüppchen Fans zum Sportplatz ziehen. Nach der zweiten Stunde waren alle Schüler und Lehrer eingeladen, den beiden Teams zuzusehen. Nach dem obligatorischen Gruppenfoto und einem kurzen Aufwärmen ertönte endlich der Anpfiff.
Sofort war klar, dass sich die Mannschaften nichts schenken würden. Herr Müller agierte allerdings sehr leichtsinnig, als er gleich in der 3. Minute den Ball nach hinten passte – direkt vor die Füße von Stefan aus der 11b, der prompt den Ball ins Tor schob.
Danach spielten die Lehrer etwas vorsichtiger und defensiver, trotzdem folgten noch zwei Tore für die Schüler. Nach einem groben Foul an Frau Weber sah Markus allerdings rot, und Frau Weber konnte den Elfmeter sicher verwandeln.
Die Halbzeitpause verging mit einem Auftritt der Schulband wie im Fluge, und nach dem hart erarbeiteten Sieg der Schüler wurden die Lehrer wie immer noch zum gemütlichen Beisammensein bei Limo und kleinen Snacks eingeladen, sodass der Vormittag in ausgelassener und fröhlicher Stimmung endete.

30

80 Gesamtpunkte 80 – 66 Punkte: ☺ 65 – 41 Punkte: 😐 40 – 0 Punkte: ☹

# People and Places in Chicago – Test 2

## 1 Reading comprehension: Al Capone

**Al Capone**

Chicago is famous for many places and many people, but the most famous of all is Al Capone. Even children know the name of this gangster. And the name is always linked to the city of Chicago.

But Al Capone was not born there – he was born in Brooklyn, New York, and he had six brothers and two sisters. His family had come from Italy and was very poor. At that time, the beginning of the 20th century, being a young boy in New York was not a very easy life.

Although he was quite clever, he left school after eighth grade and worked in different areas. At the same time he also became a member of a famous youth gang. When he was only 15 years old he had already joined a very dangerous and well-known crime gang. In 1917, when he was only 18 years old, people gave him his nickname "Scarface", after he had been hurt with a knife in a street fight. At that time he also killed a man for the first time, but the police couldn't do anything, because nobody wanted to say anything against him.

When the situation became too dangerous for him in New York, he moved on to Chicago, where he soon became one of the most important gangsters.

In the 1920ies Chicago offered many opportunities for gangsters like Al Capone. In 1920 the brewing and selling of alcohol was completely forbidden in the USA, but the people never accepted this "prohibition". And the government didn't do much to make this law accepted in public.

Alcohol was produced and sold everywhere for very much money, and the government didn't do much to control every street or river or bar. So there were a lot of gangsters who earned a lot of money by selling alcohol illegally – and one of them was Al Capone.

He became the boss of a famous and very powerful gang, and soon he became a symbol of organized crime. He was a very charming person and a good friend of the highest police officers, he was the first gangster who used the newspapers to present himself in a very good light, and he often gave money to poor people, so he was seen as a kind of modern Robin Hood. He also loved to give huge parties. For the public, he was a friendly and nice businessman who sold furniture and washed dirty clothes – he was the first gangster who invested his illegal money in laundry* services. (And the expression "money laundering" is still used today.) And he was very fair towards the men who worked for him.

But in "business" he was very brutal and cold-blooded. He killed many men when they tried to fight him, but the police could never do anything against him – and sometimes the police didn't want to do anything, because he had given them a lot of money.

It was only in 1931 that the police could arrest him and he had to go to prison for ten years – but not because he had killed many men, but because he hadn't paid his taxes*. Moreover, in 1933 alcohol became legal again. The government realized that the prohibition of alcohol didn't have the effects they had wanted: there were still many people who drank, and many people even became ill or died when they drank the illegal (and bad) alcohol. And it was due to the prohibition that mafia families or organizations like Al Capone's gang had become so powerful.

But his name is still well-known and very famous today. He is mentioned in many films and books. There is, for example, a book about a boy who is bullied at school, and when he tells his father about this, his dad cries out: "But we are not in Chicago!"

* Laundry = *Wäscherei;* taxes = *Steuer*

I. In each set of three sentences one is correct. Tick off the correct sentence!

1. ● Everybody knows who Al Capone was.
   ● Al Capone is only famous in Chicago.
   ● Al Capone is known only by children.

2. ● Al Capone was part of the government in Chicago.
   ● Al Capone committed many crimes in Chicago.
   ● Al Capone worked as a barkeeper in Chicago.

3. ● His parents had eight children.
   ● His parents had nine children.
   ● He had eight brothers.

4. ● He only went to school for nine years.
   ● He left school after the seventh year.
   ● He left school after eight years.

5. ● Growing up in New York was very hard at that time.
   ● Al Capone didn't have hard times in New York.
   ● Growing up in New York was quite easy at that time.

6. ● Al Capone was born in 1999.
   ● Al Capone was born in 1899.
   ● Al Capone was born in 1901.

7. ● He hurt somebody badly in a street fight.
   ● After a bad street fight he had a huge scar in his face.
   ● He killed somebody with a knife and cut a scar into his face.

___ / 7

II. Fill in the missing words.

When Al Capone was wanted by the police in New York, he ______________________ to Chicago. He started to sell alcohol ______________________, because at that time alcohol was completely forbidden. Many people didn't accept this, so they bought alcohol and spent a lot of money on it – and the government couldn't ______________________ them, because they couldn't control every ______________________ in the cities. So Al Capone had the opportunity to become the boss of ______________________ . Everybody in Chicago knew him, because he didn't ______________________ from the reporters and he was seen in the newspapers very often. He was also very successful in making good friends with ______________________ , and due to this many important people ______________________ him.

___ / 8

III. Complete the sentences.

1. Many people in Chicago liked him a lot, because he ________________________________________ .
2. In public he looked like a normal businessman who ________________________________________.
3. The expression "money laundering" is still used today for people

   who ____________________________________________________________________.
4. In 1931 he was caught by the police because he ________________________________________ .
5. You can see that he is still very famous today, because ____________________________________ .

5

## 2 Vocabulary: the Black Socks scandal

Fill in the missing words. The German translations are given below in the box, but not in the correct order.

**angeben • einkaufen • gegen ... spielen • hintereinander • Nachteile • Niederlage • schwören • Verantwortung**

Chicago is famous for its sports teams and the city sometimes __________________________ with its baseball and basketball teams. The White Socks, for example, are a big name in baseball. But there was also a scandal about this team and they were sometimes even called "Black Socks" after that. In 1919 they __________________________ Cincinnati – and they suffered a spectacular __________________________. Because they had won ten games __________________________ before, this was a great surprise to everybody. But soon the bosses of the team found out that this was the __________________________ of eight of the players – they had gambled about the match and made a lot of money. Of course they weren't supposed to play after that – and of course they __________________________ that they had done nothing, but this didn't help them. The scandal brought great __________________________ for the team, too, because it took a long time to find new good players and to __________________________ them, which also cost them a lot of money. But today the White Sox are an awesome team again – and even Barack Obama is a great fan of theirs.

8

## 3 Grammar: simple past/present perfect

Fill in the verb in the simple past or in the present perfect.

Tony and Marvin are working on a Wendella boat.

**Tony**: Hi Marvin, (1) ______________________ (you – already – clean) the floors this morning?

**Marvin**: Yes, and it was necessary, too. Yesterday some tourists (2) ______________________ (walk) around with dirty shoes.

**Tony**: Look! There is our new leaflet about the history of the Wendella boats!

**Marvin**: I (3) ______________________ (see) it ~~already~~. The boss (4) ______________________ (give) me one last week. And I like it much better than the old one!

**Tony**: And the pictures are all new – a friend of mine (5) ______________________ (take) them last year. Just look at the skyline!

5

## 4 Grammar: present perfect progressive

Fill in the verb in the present perfect simple or the present perfect progressive.

John (1) ______________________ (just – finish) his work for today at the huge ferris wheel on Navy Pier. He must still tidy up. He (2) ______________________ (work) there for eight years, so he knows what he must do. Today he (3) ______________________ (find) a bag in one of the cabins. It (4) ______________________ (do) turns on the wheel for hours! Thanks to that it is very difficult to give it back. He (5) ______________________ (not – clean) the floor of the entrance yet, but he (6) ______________________ (clean) the cabins – for two hours! So he's very tired now.

6

## 5 Grammar: mixed tenses

Fill in the verb in the correct tense.

Chicago is also famous for Blues music. Every year a big festival takes place near Lake Michigan. Many famous bands (1) ______________________ (invite) this year, and most of them are very happy to come. Last year some bands (2) ______________________ (not – play), because the weather was really bad. When the festival (3) ______________________ (start), it

(4) ______________________ (rain) very hard, so many people just (5) ______________________ (leave). But the year before that the weather (6) ______________________ (be) great. Karl wants to go there this year. He (7) ______________________ (find) a leaflet with the program, and he (8) ______________________ (read) it right now. He (9) ______________________ (buy) the tickets next week, and he is sure he (10) ______________________ (have) a good time. Laura (11) ______________________ (come), too, although she doesn't like Blues music very much. But she will enjoy the festival anyway.

___ / 11

## 6 Text production: email

Nick's friend Taylor from New York has asked him to write an email about his new host brother Karl. Nick wants to tell him about one place they have visited together, one difference between American and German schools and what he thinks about soccer.
Write Nick's email (about 150 words).

______________________________________________________________________

______________________________________________________________________

______________________________________________________________________

______________________________________________________________________

______________________________________________________________________

______________________________________________________________________

______________________________________________________________________

______________________________________________________________________

______________________________________________________________________

______________________________________________________________________

______________________________________________________________________

______________________________________________________________________

___ / 30

80–66 Punkte: ☺ 65–41 Punkte: 😐 40–0 Punkte: ☹ Gesamtpunkte ___ / 80

## Working with words

### 1 Wordsearch

Find the English words or expressions for the German words given below.

| | | | | | | | | | | | | | | |
|---|---|---|---|---|---|---|---|---|---|---|---|---|---|---|
| A | C | E | N | T | S | E | B | H | I | N | S | T | E | G |
| H | N | E | A | B | U | S | E | A | S | T | M | E | N | S |
| E | S | T | I | B | I | L | N | S | V | A | G | S | O | M |
| N | O | V | E | S | C | A | P | E | S | T | L | I | C | K |
| T | N | A | R | B | I | V | S | A | T | P | A | M | E | S |
| C | I | N | O | R | D | E | R | T | O | O | C | M | S | T |
| A | B | C | S | H | E | M | S | T | R | I | K | I | N | G |
| B | N | I | S | T | C | H | V | A | S | N | T | G | E | S |
| N | O | E | V | I | L | S | T | C | A | T | O | R | I | V |
| C | H | N | R | E | S | A | B | K | N | C | K | A | M | T |
| T | O | T | I | S | H | C | M | E | N | S | T | N | E | I |
| V | I | S | B | O | U | M | V | O | S | A | N | T | R | S |

Angriff • um ... zu • pulsierend, lebendig (a ... city) • alt, antik (an ... site) • Mangel • auf etwas zeigen (to ... to) • schlecht, böse • Einwanderer • auffällig (a ... feature) • Selbstmord • entkommen • Missbrauch • Sklave

### 2 Describing pictures: Thanksgiving

Fill in the gaps in order to describe the picture.

1. There is a big table ______________________________ of the picture.
2. ______________________________ of the picture you can see a group of Europeans.
3. On the other side, ______________________________ of the picture, there is a group of Native Americans.
4. ______________________________ there is a turkey who is looking at the viewer.
5. ______________________________ there are some trees.
6. There is a bird ______________________________.
7. ______________________________ of the picture I can see the sun shining in the sky.
8. And there is a little dog ______________________________ of the picture.

## Grammar: the passive voice and different tenses

Für die **Verwendung der Zeitformen** im Passiv gelten genau die gleichen Regeln wie für die Zeitformen im Aktiv.
Im Passiv wird die jeweilige Zeitform immer mit der Form von *to be* ausgedrückt, das *past participle* bleibt immer gleich. Auch die *progressive*-Formen können im Passiv gebildet werden, sind aber nur sehr selten zu finden.
• *see also TB p. 165*

Im Unterschied zum Deutschen können im Englischen aus einem Aktiv-Satz mit zwei Objekten auch zwei Passivsätze gebildet werden. Zum Beispiel:
**Aktivsatz:** *The Indians gave the Europeans food.*
**Passivsatz 1**: *Food was given to the Europeans (by the Indians).* → direktes Objekt wird zum Subjekt
**Passivsatz 2**: *The Europeans were given food (by the Indians).* → indirektes Objekt wird zum Subjekt

### 3 The passive voice: different tenses

Fill in the passive forms of the verbs in the correct tense.

1. Before every rodeo competition, Taylor ______________________________ (tell) what he must do by his coach.
2. The horses ______________________________ (give) food by the riders.
3. Last year one rider broke his leg. He ______________________________ (take) to hospital immediately.

4. Up to then, nobody ______________________ (hurt) so badly during a rodeo competition.

5. So Taylor will be very careful. After all, he wants to win so that he ______________________ (give) the prize!

## 4 The passive voice: infinitives with or without *to*

Grundsätzlich lautet die **Form des Infinitivs im Passiv** immer *be* zusammen mit dem *past participle* des Verbs.

Ob vor dem Infinitiv ein *to* steht oder nicht, hängt davon ab, was **vor** dem *be* steht:
Nach Modalverben, die ohne *to* verwendet werden, wird auch im Passiv kein *to* verwendet.
*The visitors **can see** the horses clearly from every seat.* (Aktiv)
*The horses **can be seen** clearly from every seat.* (Passiv)

Nach Modalverben oder Verben, die eine Erwartung ausdrücken (*hope, expect, ask, want, like* etc.), wird sowohl im Aktiv als auch im Passiv ein *to* vor den Infinitiv gestellt.
*Taylor hopes that his friends will support him.* (Aktiv)
*Taylor hopes to be supported by his friends.* (Passiv)
Meistens ist diese letztere Form auch die elegantere Ausdrucksweise.

Circle the right form in the following sentences.

1. Taylor hopes (to be given/to give/be given) a rodeo scholarship.
2. So the competition must (be won/be winning/to be win) by him.
3. He expects (be looked down on/to be looked down on/to be looking down on) after a defeat.
4. The horses can (be left/to be left/be leave) alone only for a short time.
5. They like (be looked/be look/to be looked after) by their riders.

## 5 Past perfect simple/progressive

Wie du bereits weißt, wird das **past perfect** für eine Handlung verwendet, die **vor einem bekannten Zeitpunkt in der Vergangenheit** stattgefunden hat.
Auch bei dieser Zeit wird unterschieden zwischen dem
• **simple**, bei dem das Ergebnis im Vordergrund steht, und dem
• **progressive**, bei dem die Handlung selbst bzw. ihre Dauer im Vordergrund steht.
*Taylor arrived at the competition very early. He had started from home one hour before.*
→ past perfect simple: Die Dauer spielt keine Rolle bzw. ist bei ***started*** keine länger andauernde Handlung.
*When Taylor was called up for his competition, he had been sitting around for an hour.*
→ past perfect progressive: Die Dauer bzw. die Handlung selbst wird betont.

Fill in the past perfect simple or the past perfect progressive.

Sehr oft wird das **past perfect progressive** (wie das **present perfect progressive**) zusammen mit einer Zeitangabe verwendet, zum Beispiel *for seven years*, *since Monday*, *since 2010*, *for 10 minutes*.

When Taylor came home after the competition, he ...

1. ____________________ (pack) all the things into his bag.
2. ____________________ (look after) his horse for half an hour.
3. ____________________ (talk) to his coach for ten minutes.
4. ____________________ (forget) to buy his girlfriend a little present.
5. ____________________ (thank) all his friends who ____________________ (support) him for more than two hours.

## Reading/Listening

### 6 Sacajawea

**Sacajawea**

If you read books about the Wild West or watch Western movies, you might get the impression that there were only men. It is true that there were many more men than women when the settlers moved west, but of course there were some women, too.

Most women were the wives of cowboys or gold diggers, and they were highly respected. There were also some women who worked in the bars or saloons. And very few women tried to live their own life and behaved like men – they hunted animals, drank alcohol, used swearwords in public and loved gambling in the saloons.

One woman, however, played a very important role in the settlement of the West: Sacajawea.

This young woman was born in a Shoshone tribe, but she was kidnapped by another tribe and sold to a French trapper when she was about 13 years old. This French man worked for the first expedition with Lewis and Clark across the Rocky Mountains. Whereas her husband wasn't of much use for the expedition, Sacajawea saved the members' lives more than just once.

When they met Native Americans, she could talk to them – and convince them not to attack. And when the men couldn't find anything to eat anymore, it was she who showed them where to find food. Once a bag with important instruments fell into a river – and again it was she who jumped after it, while the men were standing around. Finally they even met her own tribe – and from that moment on it was easy for them to buy new horses.

At the end of the expedition she was seen as the most important member of the group, and she is still honored today as a person who had great influence on the westward movement in America. In 1963, the Native Indians of Wind River reservation in Wyoming even built a monument for her – although it is not sure that she returned there after the expedition.

Tick off the correct statements.

- In the Wild West there were nearly as many women as men.
- Some women were married to cowboys.
- Some women could even shoot brilliantly.
- Sacajawea was one of the women who behaved like men.
- Sacajawea's husband was the leader of the first expedition across the Rocky Mountains.
- She could speak with the Indians and stop them when they planned an attack.
- It was her job on the expedition to cook for the men.
- She was not very brave, but the men in the expedition helped her.
- During the expedition she met her own family.
- Without her the expedition would not have been successful.
- The Native Americans of the Wind River reservation in Wyoming are very proud of her.
- It's a fact that she spent her last years there in Wyoming.

## 7 College rodeo

Fill in the missing words.

1. Trevor and Marty met during the Rodeo Competition ____________________ ago.
2. Marty has been given the scholarship for Tarleton ____________________.
3. It is quite ____________________ to go to college with a scholarship.
4. The team spirit is great, so there will be no ____________________ if you fall off a bull.
5. Rachel Hendrix had been taking part in rodeos for ____________________.
6. The scholarship is awarded to ______________________________ each year.
7. You must be a member of a ______________________________ Association.
8. You must also show that you take part in ____________________ activities.
9. That's no problem for Taylor, because he ____________________ with horses and knows everybody in Douglas.
10. Taylor is ____________________ that he comes from a town like Douglas.

## Text production

### 8 Analyzing pictures

Write a short text (about 150 words) which describes and explains the following picture showing life in a reservation today.
Refer to the setting and the situation, the people and objects you can see, your background knowledge about the topic and your personal opinion. Use your exercise book.

Folgende **Leitfragen** sollten bei der Bearbeitung dieser Aufgabe berücksichtigt werden:
- Habe ich alle Gegebenheiten des Bildes in ihren Zusammenhängen beschrieben?
- Habe ich die Informationen dabei sinnvoll aufgebaut, zum Beispiel vom Allgemeinen ausgehend hin zu den Details?
- Habe ich Zusammenhänge hergestellt und nicht nur aufgezählt?
- Habe ich anhand des Kontexts (Titel oder Überschrift, Entstehungszeit, Urheber) und meines Hintergrundwissens erklärt, was zu sehen ist?
- Habe ich als Zusammenfassung geklärt, welche Haltung das Bild gegenüber dem Thema ausdrückt?
- Habe ich in einem Schlusssatz kurz wiedergegeben, wie ich selbst diese Haltung finde?
- Ist die Bildanalyse sprachlich korrekt verfasst?

Gehe dazu auch die Leitfragen im Vorwort (S. 8) durch.

### 9 Debate

You are doing an online debate with your partner school in Douglas, Wyoming.
The topic at the moment is:
Should there be day off for all students at the High School to watch the rodeo with the school team?
Write your contribution in answer to Marty's statement (about 150 words).
Refer to two aspects which support your opinion!
Use your exercise book.

**Marty**: I'm absolutely convinced that watching a rodeo is a great thing for everybody! After all, rodeo is not a sport for single people, but you also see a lot about how to look after animals, about how to work with nature, about how to work together in a team. When you watch a complete rodeo tournament, you learn a lot about the horses – what they eat, how they react on people, what they like and what they hate. Today many young people don't know anything about animals. So why shouldn't they go to a rodeo and learn a lot there instead of sitting in a classroom?

Eine Debatte wird in der Regel **mündlich** geführt. Dennoch gibt es inzwischen viele Gelegenheiten, die Techniken der Debatte auch schriftlich anzuwenden – vor allem im Internet. Folgende Leitfragen solltest du bei einem schriftlichen Debattenbeitrag beachten:

- Bin ich auf die vorhergehende Äußerung eingegangen, indem ich sie kurz wiederhole und dann kommentiere?
- Habe ich zwei sinnvolle und überzeugende Gründe gefunden, die meine Meinung unterstützen?
- Habe ich bei diesen Gründen klar genannt, was die Behauptung ist? Wird dann auch erklärt, inwiefern diese Behauptung wichtig ist? Habe ich Beispiele oder Beweise ergänzt, mit denen meine Gründe überzeugend werden?
- Habe ich sprachliche Strategien angewandt, um meine Meinung überzeugend zu gestalten? Habe ich zum Beispiel Fragen gestellt, einzelne wichtige Begriffe wiederholt, den Satzbau von kurzen Sätzen wiederholt oder besonders lebendige Wörter verwendet?
- Habe ich einen klaren Gedankengang aufgebaut?
- Habe ich den Debattenbeitrag sprachlich richtig verfasst?

Gehe dazu auch die Leitfragen im Vorwort (S. 8) durch.

## 10 Newspaper article

Write a short newspaper article about Thanksgiving in the USA from a German's point of view (about 150 words).
Use your background information and the facts and pictures given on p. 34/35 in your text-book to write about two different aspects!
Use your exercise book.

Ein Zeitungsartikel muss nicht lang, sollte aber (wie auch ein Artikel in der Schülerzeitung) spannend und lebendig sein!
Stelle dir also folgende Fragen:

- Habe ich eine packende, knackige Überschrift gefunden?
- Habe ich den Text in Absätze eingeteilt?
- Wird im ersten Absatz deutlich, um welches Ereignis es geht bzw. was die Hauptaussage ist?
- Habe ich auch persönliche Eindrücke oder Ansichten einbezogen?
- Habe ich die vorhandenen Informationen verwendet und mit eigenen Ideen ergänzt?
- Habe ich die Informationen dadurch lebendig wiedergegeben, dass ich Beispiele nenne, eine Geschichte mit einer unerwarteten Wendung erzähle, Betroffene oder Experten zitiere oder über die Hintergründe spekuliere?
- Ist der Artikel sprachlich richtig verfasst?

Gehe dazu auch die Leitfragen im Vorwort (S. 8) durch.

Zeit: 45 min Beginn Ende

# Pocahontas – Test 1

## 1 Reading comprehension: Pocahontas

**Pocahontas**

When asked about the most famous tragic lovers in the world, most people will answer "Romeo and Juliet" – but some may also say "Pocahontas and Captain Smith". It was not only the Disney movie of 1995 that made this beautiful Indian girl and her handsome British lover popular in the world. This love story had been well-known for nearly 400 years.

Pocahontas was born as an Indian princess in 1595. Her father Powhatan, chief of an Algonquin tribe, loved her very much, although she was not his only daughter. He asked her when there were problems, so she had great influence on him.

She was still a young girl when the Europeans first landed in the part of America that became the state of Virginia later. One expedition was led by the Englishman John Smith in 1607. It was then that the Algonquin tribe saw Europeans for the first time, and Powhatan and his daughter Pocahontas didn't agree about what to do. Pocahontas was convinced that the "strangers" and the Algonquin could live together in peace, so that they could learn from the other cultures. So she helped and supported the Europeans: she taught them where to find food and also the language of her tribe. Her father, however, didn't want to have the Europeans on his country. He fought against them and tried to move them away from his country.

It was during this conflict that the story of Pocahontas and Captain Smith was born. When he returned to England later, he reported that Pocahontas had saved his life. When her father had tried to shoot him, she had thrown herself in front of him and so risked her own life.

But does this really mean that she was in love with him? We only have Captain Smith's report about the event, and this was given only years later. And he wanted to be seen in a very good light, so maybe he exaggerated a bit. After all, he was 15 years older than Pocahontas, and he had been in many wars in Europe already. And maybe Pocahontas just wanted to stop the fighting and bring peace to her own tribe and the Europeans.

In 1613, however, the Englishmen caught her and she had to stay with them. She was brought to the new settlement of Jamestown and she also became a Christian. We still don't know if she had wanted this or if the Englishmen – including John Smith – had forced her. From that moment on she gave up her Indian name and was called Rebecca. This name was seen as very appropriate for her by the Europeans, because it means "the mother of two nations".

One year later she married the farmer John Rolfe, one of the settlers near Jamestown, but this took place thanks to politics, not due to love – a very typical phenomenon at that time. And she was successful in her plans: after that there was peace between the Algonquin Indians and the European settlers in their new town Jamestown for several years.

Pocahontas – now Rebecca Rolfe – then went to England in 1615, when the English king invited her to his court. She was the only Native American who was invited, and she was the only girl who was seen as a princess. In England she soon became very popular and everybody tried to be her friend, because she was very intelligent, beautiful and also exotic. It was also in England that she died one year later. Her traces, however, can still be seen today. Her son Thomas, who was born in 1615, left a huge family, and still today many Americans are very proud to be a member of her family. The most famous one is the former American president George W. Bush. And she is one of the only two women who have ever been pictured on US banknotes. So when Disney released the film in 1995 everybody knew about her, and although the love story is not true, she is still considered to be one of the most fascinating characters in American history.

I. Are the statements right or wrong?

| | | right | wrong |
|---|---|---|---|
| 1. | Pocahontas and Captain Smith are an example of tragic lovers. | ● | ● |
| 2. | The story happened around 1700. | ● | ● |
| 3. | Pocahontas didn't have any brothers or sisters. | ● | ● |
| 4. | Before Captain Smith met Pocahontas the Algonquin had never seen Europeans. | ● | ● |
| 5. | Powhatan tried to make peace with the English settlers. | ● | ● |
| 6. | Pocahontas was shot when she tried to save Captain Smith's life. | ● | ● |

6

II. Complete the text.

At the age of (1) ______________________, Pocahontas was brought to Jamestown. She became a Christian, too, and was given the name (2)______________________. The Europeans liked her new name very much, because they saw her as the person who brought peace to both the Algonquin and the (3)______________________ .

In Jamestown she also became Mrs. Rolfe, although she and her husband were not in love. At that time it was very common that people married for (4)______________________ reasons – and it was her achievement that for some years there was peace between the Native Americans and the settlers. This also made her very famous in England, and the English king invited her to visit him. All the people at the king's court in London were very (5)______________________ to her, because she was intelligent, (6)______________________ and different to them. Although she died one year later in (7)______________________, she is still well-known in America, and many people are (8)______________________ to be members of her family, like George W. Bush.

8

III. Complete the following overview over the events.

| | | |
|---|---|---|
| A | | John Smith was born. |
| B | | Pocahontas met John Smith for the first time. |

| | | |
|---|---|---|
| C | 1614 | |
| D | | Pocahontas moved to London. |
| E | 1616 | |
| F | 1995 | |

6

## 2 Vocabulary: Native Americans

Write down the missing words.

1. The first Europeans who came to America to live there – the ______________________ – didn't know anything about the new country.
2. When they moved to the West, they ______________________ new towns.
3. On their way, they met different groups of Native Americans, different ______________________.
4. The Native Americans were ______________________ friendly ______________________ helpful towards the Europeans.
5. They showed them, for example, how to hunt animals so that they could get some ______________________ to eat.
6. The Europeans tried to ______________________ the Christian religion among the Native Americans.
7. They didn't understand the Native Americans' religious ______________________.
8. But they also brought diseases to the Native Americans – a great ______________________ for the people, and many Native Americans died.
9. Later, the Native Americans were brought to reservations, where they didn't have any money and lived in great ______________________ .
10. There were no jobs, so there was a lot of ______________________ .

10

## 3 Describing pictures: Pocahontas meets Captain Smith

Fill in the gaps in order to describe the picture.

1. ______________________ you can see Pocahontas and Captain Smith.
2. There is a ship ______________________ of the picture.
3. ______________________ of the picture you can see three Native Americans.
4. ______________________ there is a rabbit.
5. On the other side, ______________________ of the picture, you can see three Europeans.

5

## 4 Grammar: passive – different tenses

Fill in the verb in the passive. Use the correct tense.

Pocahontas was very important to her father. She (1) ______________ (love) very much by him. One day he said: "Girl, where have you been? You (2) ______________ (see) by your brother near the lake You know you mustn't go there alone. You (3) ______________ (tell) a thousand times already!" Pocahontas answered: "Yes, father, I know. But I (4) ______________ (visit) by my friends yesterday, and the day before they (5) ______________ (tell) that near the lake there were such beautiful flowers! And you know that I like walking around on my own – the animals are not dangerous.

5

## 5 Grammar: passive – infinitives with or without *to*

Fill in the correct form of the infinitive with or without *to*.

In the Native Americans' families the girls were expected ______________________ (look) after by their husbands. But they could tell the men when they wanted ______________________ (leave) alone. Today, the women still ______________________ (give) only pocket money. But more and more women are asking ______________________ (give) more freedom, so that they can get a job. They still have to look after the children who should ______________________ (teach) the old traditions.

___ / 5

## 6 Grammar: past perfect simple/progressive

Fill in the verb in the past perfect simple or the past perfect progressive form.

Before Captain Smith arrived in America, ...

1. he ______________________________ (sail) for six weeks.
2. his men ______________________________ (shout) that they had seen land.
3. he ______________________________ (see – never) Native Americans before.
4. he ______________________________ (watch) out for land for two hours.
5. Pocahontas ______________________________ (live) there for many years.

___ / 5

## 7 Text production: debate

Your class is doing an online debate with a partner school in Douglas, Wyoming. The topic you discuss is: Should the town give money to the Native Americans in the Wind River reservation, or should the money be spent on a new library for the High School?
Write your contribution in answer to Marcy's statement (about 150 words).
Refer to two aspects which support your opinion.
Use your exercise book.

> **Marcy:** I have to admit that the Native Americans in Wind River still have many problems. But I'm convinced that these problems won't be solved with just a pocketful of money. So I think the money should be spent on education rather than on a program that won't be successful.

___ / 30

80 – 66 Punkte: ☺ 65 – 41 Punkte: 😐 40 – 0 Punkte: ☹ Gesamtpunkte ___ / 80

Zeit: 45 min Beginn ______ Ende ______

# Wild Wild West – Test 2

## 1 Listening comprehension: Buffalo Bill

I. Complete the sentences.

1. Buffalo Bill's real name was ______________________________________________ .
2. Buffalo Bill became famous when Ned Bundline ______________________________________ .
3. As a teenager Buffalo Bill worked for the Pony Express, where he ______________________
   ______________________________________________________________________ .
4. After the American Civil War he still was a soldier and took part in _____________________
   ______________________________________________________________________ .
5. In the battle near Summit Springs against the Cheyenne he ___________________________
   ______________________________________________________________________ .
6. Buffalo Bill also sold fresh meat to the men who ______________________________________ .
7. He was called Buffalo Bill because he __________________________________________ .

7

II. Tick off the correct statements.

9. In 1872 ...
   - Buffalo Bill wrote the play "Scouts of the Prairie".
   - Buffalo Bill was invited to play himself in "Scouts of the Prairie".
   - Ned Buntline took part in his first show.

10. Buffalo Bill's Wild West Show became very popular, because ...
    - everybody was invited to take part in it.
    - the actors seemed so real.
    - many famous cowboys or even Native Americans took part.

11. Sitting Bull's father ...
    - took him out to hunt buffalo when he was 10 years old.
    - killed a buffalo in front of his eyes.
    - was called Tatanka Yotanka.

12. In the wars against the whites ...
    - the tribes of the Sioux, the Cheyenne and others always fought alone.
    - Sitting Bull didn't have to fight.
    - Sitting Bull was the head of a huge army of Native Americans.

13. In the battle of the Little Big Horn in 1876 ...
- the Native Americans were very successful.
- the Canadians supported Sitting Bull.
- the Sioux were defeated completely.

14. When he went to Germany with his show in 1891, Buffalo Bill ...
- had already been known to many Germans.
- had a hard time to find an audience.
- caused great interest in the Wild West.

15. Although his show had been very successful in Europe,
- he was never accepted by important people.
- he lost nearly all his money after about 30 years.
- he didn't want to go back to Europe after about 30 years.

16. The small town Cody in Wyoming ...
- was founded by Buffalo Bill himself.
- even offers a Buffalo Bill hunting school.
- doesn't exist anymore.

8

III. Complete the following overview over the events.

| | | |
|---|---|---|
| A | 1846 | |
| B | | Cody began his work for the Pony Express. |
| C | 1865 | |
| D | | Cody married Louisa Frederici. |
| E | | battle against the Cheyenne near Summit Springs |

5

## 2 Vocabulary: going west

Fill in the missing words. You can find some hints below, but not in the correct order.

a feeling of very strong support – a group of people who work together for one aim – an illegal act like stealing or killing somebody – good for growing plants – group of people who live in one place – objects or parts of the land which are easy to see and recognize – the condition after too much alcohol – the days when nobody has to go to work – the middle point between extremes – the ways of the pioneers

Many towns in Wyoming are located along the old (1)____________________ of the settlers. They had built houses where they found (2)____________________ land. Today these towns often have a very close (3) ____________________ – people work and live together every day. There are not many (4) ____________________, but usually, like in every other place in the world, you can see people who get (5) ____________________ on Saturday night. The (6) ____________________ are usually celebrated with the whole family. And people often do a lot for their towns with rare (7)____________________ .They look after the (8) ____________________ or join (9) ____________________ to support their home towns. But usually the towns are very small – (10)____________________ only about 2 people live on each square kilometer (and about 50,000 live in the capital Cheyenne)!

/ 10

## 3 Describing pictures: after Little Big Horn

Fill in the gaps in order to describe the picture.

1. ______________________________ of the picture there is a river.

2. ______________________________ you can see some Native Americans who are walking through the river.

3. In front of them, in ______________________________ , you can see a pony.

4. ______________________________ there is one Native American on a horse.

5. ______________________________ there are some trees.

5

## 4 Grammar: passive – different tenses

Fill in the verb in the passive. Use the correct tense.

When Buffalo Bill went to Europe, he (1) ____________________ (greet) with loud applause. People (2) ____________________ (interest) in everything which (3) ____________________ (bring) from the "Wild West". So Buffalo Bill's show was a huge success. One day he said to Ann Oakley, a shooter: "People here are so great! I (4) ____________________ (show) around the whole town!" And Ann answered: "Yes, and I (5) ____________________ (already – ask) by four men to marry them!" Bill asked: "So what are you going to do?" And Ann replied: "I haven't decided yet."

5

## 5 Grammar: passive – infinitives with or without *to*

Fill in the passive infinitive with or without *to*.

1. Sitting Bull hoped ____________________ (see) as a great leader of his army.
2. He always wanted ____________________ (give) respect – both by the Native Americans and by the Europeans.
3. And many people agree: He ought ____________________ (name) as one of the most important Native Americans.
4. But in the reservations no monuments need to ____________________ (put) up – all Native Americans still know him today.
5. Children at school should ____________________ (tell) his history.

5

## 6 Grammar: past perfect simple/progressive

Fill in the verb in the past perfect simple or the past perfect progressive.

1. When Buffalo Bill founded Cody, he ______________________ (travel) around for many years.
2. He ______________________ (just – visit) the place for his future town when he met some friends.
3. They agreed to give him the money after he ______________________ (talk) about his plans for two hours.
4. And they were very rich – they ______________________ (find) gold.
5. They ______________________ (dig) for years!

5

## 7 Text production: newspaper article (mediation)

Write a short newspaper article about the German "Western City" (about 150 words).
Refer to two aspects why this place is worth a visit, and state your own opinion whether this place should be visited by Americans.
Use the information given below! Use your exercise book.

**Eine Runde durch den Wilden Westen**
Wolltest du schon immer ein Cowboy sein? Oder auch ein Rancher, eine Westernlady oder ein Indianer? In der Western City in Neuberg hast du die Gelegenheit, dich in allen möglichen Western-Disziplinen zu versuchen!
Bereits am Eingang erhältst du ein Heft, in dem du deine erzielten Punkte eintragen lassen kann. Du findest darin eine Übersicht über die verschiedenen Stationen. Mit dem Western-Express kannst du dann einmal um die Stadt herumfahren und dir die Stationen ansehen, während der Zugführer die Aufgaben erklärt.
Gleich die erste Station ist das berühmte Hufeisenwerfen. Wenn du damit noch kein Glück hast, beschwöre Manitou und das Eisen wird seinen Weg von allein finden! Sheriff Cody wird deine Punkte notieren.
Achtung! Gleich um die Ecke ragen die Hörner des hölzernen Bullen hinter dem Saloon hervor. Nimm das Lasso und versuche damit, den Bullen zu fangen! Cowboy Howie kann dir Tipps geben und trägt deine Punkte ein.
Auch im Indianerlager kannst du deine Geschicklichkeit zeigen. Nimm den Bogen und versuche alle drei Pfeile in die Mitte der Zielscheibe zu treffen. Wenn du das schaffst, wird Medizinmann Tohanka deine Punkte aufschreiben. Aber Vorsicht: Vielleicht hat er ja deine Pfeile verzaubert und du musst ihn erst zu einer Beschwörungszeremonie überreden! Vielleicht erfährst du bei der Zeremonie auch einiges über die Bräuche verschiedener Indianerstämme. (Diese Beschwörung findet nur statt, wenn genügend Zuschauer da sind.)
Oder liegen deine Talente eher im Messerwerfen? Trapper John wird dir seine Messer zur Verfügung stellen und deine Punkte zählen.
Falls du dann immer noch nicht genug weißt, erzählen die Museumsräume und der neue Westernfilm im Kino dir alles, was du noch wissen willst.
Viel Vergnügen bei diesem unvergesslichen Erlebnis!

30

80 Gesamtpunkte 80 – 66 Punkte: ☺ 65 – 41 Punkte: 😐 40 – 0 Punkte: ☹

## Working with words

In diesem Kapitel finden sich viele neue Wörter, mit denen du Gefühle beschreiben kannst. Lege dir (falls du das noch nicht getan hast) eine MindMap mit diesen Wörtern an und ergänze auch die Wörter, die du bisher gelernt hast! Du kannst dazu auch die Wörterlisten in deinem Textbook ab S. 202 durchgehen, indem du dir jeden Tag zum Beispiel eine Seite oder alle Wörter mit dem gleichen Anfangsbuchstaben vornimmst und die entsprechenden Wörter in der MindMap notierst.

### 1 Feelings

Cross out the odd word. Write down if the other words express positive or negative feelings.

1. frightened – worried – anxious – ecstatic: ____________________
2. exhausted – relieved – tired – frustrated: ____________________
3. hopeful – expectant – desperate – relieved: ____________________
4. pleased – delighted – amazed – annoyed: ____________________

### 2 American English/British English

Du hast bereits in den ersten Kapitel einige Unterschiede zwischen dem amerikanischen und dem britischen Englisch kennen gelernt. Wenn du das noch nicht gemacht hast, lege dir eine Übersicht über die wichtigsten Unterschiede an!

Fill in the missing words.

| German | American English | British English |
|---|---|---|
| | parking lot | |
| Pommes frites | | |
| | | shop |
| | cookie | |

## 3 The weather

Fill in the missing words.

Monday

Tuesday

Wednesday

1. On Monday the weather will be very ______________ .
2. On Tuesday the sun will still come out, but the sky will be ______________ .
3. On Wednesday we are expecting heavy ______________ .

# Grammar: gerund, sentence adverbs and comparison of adjectives

## 4 Gerund constructions

**!** Die Verben und Adjektive, nach denen eine Präposition mit Gerund (*ing*-Form) steht, musst du lernen!
Am besten merkst du dir immer ein *doing* an Stelle des Gerunds, zum Beispiel be *keen on doing*, *feel like doing*, *look forward to doing* etc.

Circle the correct form.

1. Sinead and Catriona talk **about going/to go/on going** to Ellis Island.
2. Catriona has always looked forward **to see/to seeing/at seeing** the place where the immigrants arrived in the New World.
3. She insists **to visit/on visiting/about visiting** the place.
4. Sinead is tired **to go/on going/of going** to all the tourists' places.
5. But she knows that Ellis Island is a good place **for finding/to finding/of finding** information on one's own family.

## 5 Gerund or infinitive?

Bei den Verben *to remember*, *to try* und *to stop* verändert sich die Bedeutung, je nachdem, ob ein Gerund oder ein Infinitiv folgt.

Merke dir Beispielsätze!

Etwa zu *to stop*:
*He stopped smoking.*
*He walked down the road, then he stopped to smoke.*

Fill in the verb in the gerund or in the infinitive.

1. On her last day in New York, Catriona remembered ____________________ (buy) some souvenirs for her friends back home.
2. So she and Sinead went shopping. But after half an hour they stopped ____________________ (drink) some coke.
3. Catriona always tried ____________________ (use) the American words, but everybody noticed that she was Irish.
4. But she never stopped ____________________ (imitate) the American accent.
5. And even one year later Sinead remembered ____________________ (teach) her new words.

## 6 Sentence adverbs

Circle the expression which is more appropriate.

Lege dir eine Übersicht über diese Art von Adverben und Satzteilen an und verwende sie möglichst oft, wenn du selbst etwas schreibst! Damit kannst du die Texte gut strukturieren.

Catriona and Sinead want to go shopping.

1. **First of all/Immediately** they think about the shops they want to visit.
2. **Afterwards/Finally** they put on their coats and leave the house.
3. **Just when/In the meantime**, when they arrive at Macy's, Sinead notices that she has forgotten to take some money with her.
4. They return home **immediately/later**.

## 7 Revision: questions

Auch bei **Fragen** bleibt die übliche **Wortstellung Subjekt–Verb–Objekt** erhalten: Gehört zum Verb ohnehin schon ein Hilfsverb, wird dieses vor das Subjekt gestellt, ansonsten wird dafür die entsprechende Form von *to do* verwendet.
Wenn die Frage ein **Fragewort** enthält, folgt das Hilfverb auf das Fragewort. Eine Ausnahme gibt es nur bei dem Fragewort *who*, wenn dieses das Subjekt des Satzes ist.
*Who goes shopping?*

Eine Besonderheit sind ***question tags***, die an einen Aussagesatz angehängt werden, wenn man mit Zustimmung rechnet – also bei Sätzen, in denen im Deutschen ein *oder*? angehängt wird.

Bei einem bejahten Aussagesatz wird die verneinte Form des Hilfsverbs (bzw. die entsprechende Form von *to do*) mit dem Subjekt des Satzes angehängt.
Bei einem verneinten Aussagesatz wird die bejahte Frage angehängt.
*Catriona and Sinead are cousins, **aren't they**?*
*They haven't met before, **have they**?*
*They love shopping, **don't they**?*

Write down the complete questions.

1. Catriona: **Where** ____________________

   Sinead: We can get something to drink in that bar over there.

2. Sinead: **Do** ____________________

   Catriona: Yes, I like New York very much.

3. Sinead: **Can** ____________________

   Catriona: No, I can't. I can't stay here for two more weeks, because I have to go back to school.

Complete the questions by adding the question tag.

4. Catriona: You'll go to the choir tonight, ________________?
5. Sinead: Yes. And you can come with me, ________________?
6. Catriona: That sounds great, ________________?
7. Catriona: The girls in the choir are nice, ________________?
8. Sinead: Yeah. You have met a lot of nice people here, ________________?
9. Catriona: We always meet many great people, ________________?
10. New York is full of really fascinating people, ________________?

## 8 Revision: comparison of adjectives

Wenn du Dinge **vergleichen** willst, musst du folgende Regeln beachten:
- Bei **einsilbigen** Adjektiven wird *-er/-est* angehängt (*cool – cooler – coolest*).
- **Zweisilbige** Adjektive, die auf *-y* enden, werden mit *-ier/-iest* gesteigert, dafür entfällt das *-y* (*funny – funnier – funniest*).
- Adjektive mit **drei und mehr** Silben werden mit *more/most* gesteigert (*interesting – more interesting – most interesting*).

Unregelmäßige Formen finden sich bei *good – better – best* und *bad – worse – worst*.

Fill in the adjective in the comparative (+) or the superlative (++)!

1. Catriona thinks that New York is the ______________ (good ++) city in the world.
2. She likes the christmas tree in front of Rockefeller Center a lot – it's ________________ (gigantic +) than any other tree she has ever seen.
3. And she likes the girls in Sinead's choir. She thinks they are much ________________ (friendly +) than the boys.

## Reading/Listening

## 9 Central Park

This is part of Catriona's email to her friend in Ireland. Read it first.

Yesterday we did something really great: We went to Central Park. You should have seen us in our coats – it was freezing, although there were no clouds and the sky was clear and blue. So the weather was ideal for us. We just walked around a bit – two of 35 million visitors who come each year! Just imagine that! And Sinead showed me some of the really famous parts of the park. Unfortunately it was too cold to watch some guys who were playing baseball ... ☺
This was on the Great Lawn. It is a huge field in the middle of the park. You can go there to relax or do sports like baseball and basketball. And if you love listening to music, you can even visit free concerts on the Great Lawn in summer!
Afterwards, we walked past the Strawberry Fields area, which got its name after John Lennon, the famous member of the Beatles, who was killed in 1980 right in front of his apartment near Central Park, in the famous Dakota building. He had loved Central Park and often stayed in one area, and his fans remembered meeting him there. So this place was given the name "Strawberry Fields", an expression taken from one of his songs, as a symbol of peace. Many fans still go there every day to bring flowers, poems or candles. You know his song "Imagine", don't you?

Are the statements right or wrong? Tick off the correct box.

| | | right | wrong |
|---|---|---|---|
| 1. | Catriona didn't enjoy her visit to Central Park very much, because it was too cold. | ● | ● |
| 2. | It was very cold, and there were many clouds. | ● | ● |
| 3. | You can play baseball in Central Park. | ● | ● |
| 4. | There were 35 million people there with her. | ● | ● |
| 5. | If you want to play basketball, you have to go to the Great Lawn. | ● | ● |
| 6. | Free concerts are held in the Strawberry Fields. | ● | ● |
| 7. | John Lennon called one part of Central Park "Strawberry Fields". | ● | ● |
| 8. | "Strawberry Fields" is very popular with Lennon's fans. | ● | ● |

## 10 Christmas shopping

Listen to the conversation between Marvin and his friend Tobey.
Complete the sentences.

1. Marvin doesn't have a present for his sister Katrina yet, because ____________________

   ____________________________________________.

2. Tobey doesn't want to buy a scarf, because ____________________

   ____________________________________________.

3. They won't go to a book store, because ____________________

   ____________________________________________.

4. Marvin doesn't want to buy tickets for the new Christmas musical, because ____________________

   ____________________________________________.

5. Marvin likes the idea of going to Macy's, because ____________________

   ____________________________________________.

6. Tobey wants to go to the Rockefeller Center, because ____________________

   ____________________________________________.

7. Tobey wants to have a cup of hot cider first, because ____________________

   ____________________________________________.

## Text production

### 11 Online chat

!

Bei einem **Chat** kommt es (wie bei einer E-Mail) darauf an, wer angesprochen wird – danach richtet sich sowohl der Inhalt als auch die verwendete Sprache. Im Unterschied zur E-Mail sind die formalen Vorgaben aber weniger genau.
Stelle dir für einen Dialog folgende **Leitfragen**:
- Habe ich Inhalte gefunden, die meinen Gesprächspartner interessieren?
- Habe ich immer den Gesprächspartner im Blick, indem ich Bezug auf ihn nehme und auf seine Äußerungen reagiere?
- Habe ich einen passenden Ton getroffen?
- Ist die E-Mail sprachlich richtig verfasst?

Gehe dazu auch die Leitfragen im Vorwort (S. 8) durch.

Catriona is chatting with her friend Maureen in Ireland. Maureen wants to know about Catriona's experiences of Christmas shopping in New York and tells Catriona about the christmas market back home.
Write the dialogue (about 150 words). Use your exercise book.

### 12 Audio guide

Sinead's school is doing a project on "the other side" of New York – the parts where tourists usually don't go. They are working on an audio guide for teenagers. Sinead has promised to do a chapter on Asian immigrants in New York. Write her script for the audio guide (about 150 words). Use your erxercise book.
Use the photo on p. 66 and the charts on p. 69 in your book.

!

Wie bei einem Artikel für die Schülerzeitung soll ein **Audio Guide** spannend und lebendig sein. Im Unterschied zum schriftlichen Zeitungsartikel sollte aber noch viel mehr beschrieben werden – was man sehen, hören, riechen oder fühlen kann, sollte immer auch mit Worten ausgedrückt werden.
Stelle dir also folgende **Leitfragen**:
- Habe ich mit abwechslungsreichen Adjektiven oder Zitaten den Text lebendig gestaltet?
- Habe ich die Informationen anschaulich beschrieben und einbezogen?
- Habe ich persönliche Eindrücke einbezogen?
- Ist der Audio Guide sprachlich richtig verfasst?

Gehe dazu auch die Leitfragen im Vorwort (S. 8) durch.

Zeit: 45 min Beginn Ende

## Ellis Island – Test 1

### 1 Reading comprehension: famous immigrants

**Ellis Island – and then?**

Everybody knows Annie Moore, and she was only a teenager. She was the first immigrant to pass Ellis Island, her statue is still there. But there are other people, too, who had to pass Ellis Island to start a new life in the New World – and some of them became famous and their names are still known today.

There is, for example, Max Factor, whose company is well-known among girls and women around the whole world. He was born as Maksymilian Faktorowicz in Poland in the 1870s, and he started working for a make-up artist and hairdresser when he was only nine years old. At that time, this job was very important, especially for the kings and queens in "old Europe", and also for the theatres. He went to Moscow and Berlin, and soon, when he was still very young, he worked for the European royals. At the beginning of the 20th century he and his whole family decided to emigrate to the USA, and he kept on working in his job. In 1904 he showed his talent in America for the first time in a huge exhibition, before he moved to Los Angeles in 1908. There he founded the company Max Factor – and he became famous, because at that time the film industry in Hollywood was just starting. So when he started to develop his own make-up for Hollywood in 1914, he soon became very popular with the actors. And his influence on the beauty industry can still be seen today: he invented expressions like "make-up" or beauty products like waterproof mascara and, in 1930, lipgloss.

Another name that is well-known around the world is Maria Trapp. This woman was born in Austria in 1905 and at first she wanted to join a convent and become a nun – she was very religious. At the age of 20 she was sent to the house of a well-known and respected captain, Georg von Trapp, whose wife had died and left him with seven children. But it was like in a Hollywood romance: they fell in love and married. She was very musical and sang a lot with the children, who loved her very much. They even took part in some concerts. When the family lost all their money in 1935, she had the idea of founding a choir with the family. Soon the Trapp family became very famous and popular, and they even won several prizes. In 1938 the political situation in Austria changed, and the family had to emigrate – and came to Ellis Island. From there, they started to give concerts and toured the USA and later even South America and Australia. And people respected them a lot, because after the 2nd World War they organized help for the poor people in Austria. When in 1959 the story of the family was turned into a Broadway musical and a film – "The Sound of Music" – they became famous in all the world. The musical was very popular, and even today everybody knows it. Most Americans can sing along to the songs even today. The Trapp family was even given a medal of honour by the Austrian city of Salzburg, because after the movie many more tourists came to visit Salzburg. The musical tells the story of the emigration in a very dramatic way. But of course the story is exaggerated, because they didn't have to escape at night, but left Europe very openly by train. Maria Trapp died at the age of 82 in 1987.

And there is a third name that most people in all the world know: Rudolph Valentino. He came to New York to start a new life at the age of 20 as a very poor man. He hadn't been able to find any job in Italy.

From Ellis Island and New York he moved to California, took part in many films and became a star in the 1920s. He even worked together with great actors of his time like Charlie Chaplin or Douglas Fairbanks. All the women loved him, the men however were not really happy about his movies. When he died in 1926 in New York, he was only 31 years old. About 100,000 people were in the streets of New York City to pay their respects, it is even reported that some women killed themselves because their idol was dead. Windows were broken in and for one day there was chaos all over the city. More than 100 police officers on horses couldn't calm down the crowds.

I. Complete the timeline.

| | | |
|---|---|---|
| A | ~ 1870 | Max Factor ________________ in Poland. |
| B | ~ 1879 | Max Factor started ____________________________________________. |
| C | 1908 | 1908 Max Factor went _____________________________. |
| D | 1914 | Max Factor started to produce ___________________________________. |
| E | 1930 | Max Factor invented _______________. |

5

II. Are the statements right or wrong?

| | | right | wrong |
|---|---|---|---|
| 1. | Georg von Trapp had already been married when he met Maria. | ● | ● |
| 2. | Georg von Trapp had six children when he met Maria. | ● | ● |
| 3. | Maria and the Trapp children became good friends. | ● | ● |
| 4. | Maria and the captain married. | ● | ● |
| 5. | Maria and the children started to perform as a choir only because they loved music so much. | ● | ● |
| 6. | When in 1938 the political situation changed in Austria, the "Trapp family" were just touring the USA. | ● | ● |
| 7. | The Trapp family never forgot their home country Austria and even supported the Austrians after the war. | ● | ● |
| 8. | The family performed their story on Broadway. | ● | ● |
| 9. | The film "The Sound of Music" was watched by many people, and many people still like it today. | ● | ● |
| 10. | The film tells the real story of the Trapp family, but in an exaggerated way. | ● | ● |

10

III. Complete the sentences.

1. When Rudolph Valentino arrived at Ellis Island, he didn't have ______________________________ .
2. He became famous after he took part ________________________________ .
3. Although the men didn't like him, the women thought __________________________________ .

4. After his death in 1926 the streets of New York were filled ______________________________ .

5 5. Even the police couldn't stop the fans who ______________________________ .

## 2 Vocabulary: arriving at Ellis Island

Fill in the missing English words! The German translations are given below, but not in the correct order.

**Angestellte • Berühmtheiten • hauptsächlich • hervorrufen • inzwischen • Minderheit • verbessern • verschwinden • widerwillig • zwingen**

The immigrants who arrived at Ellis Island were (1) _______________ poor people. Most of them had been members of a (2) _______________ in their home countries. But of course there were also rich and famous (3) _______________ among the immigrants. They, however, had enough money to (4) _______________ in the streets of New York after their arrival – at least that is what people said. (5) _______________, the poorer people were brought to the registration halls. They were usually very (6) _______________ when they had to climb up 50 steps, because they knew they were already being watched by doctors. And the (7) _______________ at Ellis Island were usually no great help. The noise, the rooms, the crowds – all this must have (8) _______________ a very frightening atmosphere! Some of the immigrants, mostly those who seemed to be ill, were (9) _______________ to stay on their ships for several days. And even if the halls were (10) _______________ in the later
10 years of Ellis Island, the experience must have been horrible.

## 3 Vocabulary: How did they feel?

Fill in a synonym for the underlined word. The first letter is already given.

1. Many immigrants felt very lonely and i_______________ when they arrived at Ellis Island.
2. And of course they were frightened and a_______________ when they started their new lives.
3. Usually the atmosphere was very awful and g_______________ at Ellis Island.
4. And after the long journey they were tired and e_______________.

5. But for those who could pass Ellis Island the trouble was over, and they felt optimistic and r________________.

5

## 4 Grammar: gerund constructions

Fill in the verbs in the correct form. Add the preposition where necessary.

1. The immigrants were all keen ____________________ (start) a new life in the USA.
2. Some of them were also looking forward ____________________ (meet) their family members who had already settled there.
3. But they usually were tired ________________ (travel) around, so they stayed in New York at first.
4. They were worried ____________________ (find) a job, however, so many moved on later.
5. But most of the immigrants never forgot ________________ (spend) time at Ellis Island.

5

## 5 Grammar: questions

When Annie Moore arrived at Ellis Island with her brothers, one of them had a lot of questions. Complete the questions by writing down the question tag.

1. "We can leave the ship now, ________________ ?"
2. "Mum and Dad won't find us in this huge building, ________________ ?"
3. "That doctor over there looks very strict, ________________ ?"
4. "The woman we met on the ship has got two children, ________________ ?"
5. "They have left the ship, too, ________________ ?"

5

## 6 Grammar: comparison of adjectives

Fill in the adjectives in the correct form.

For Annie Moore everything was different in New York:

1. Finding your way through the city was ____________________ (difficult) than at home.
2. But the people were ________________ (friendly) than she had thought.
3. The first days were __________________ (exciting) than everything she had experienced before.
4. And the food was ok – the food on the ship had been ________________ (bad).

5. When at last her parents found her and her brothers, it was the ____________ (precious) moment in her life.

5

## 7 Text production: audio guide

In your class you have prepared a little exhibition on sights in New York. Now you are going to add an audio guide for it, too. You have chosen the part about Ellis Island.

Write down the text for your part of the audio guide (about 150 words). Refer to the five photos that are shown in the exhibition (and on p. 62 in your textbook) and to your background knowledge!

______________________________________________

______________________________________________

______________________________________________

______________________________________________

______________________________________________

______________________________________________

______________________________________________

______________________________________________

______________________________________________

______________________________________________

______________________________________________

______________________________________________

______________________________________________

______________________________________________

30

80 Gesamtpunkte 80 – 65 Punkte: ☺ 64 – 41 Punkte: 😐 40 – 0 Punkte: ☹

Zeit: 45 min Beginn ______ Ende ______

# Christmas in New York– Test 2

## 1 Listening comprehension: Christmas shopping

I. Complete the sentences.

1. There are Macy's stores in _______________ states of the United States.
2. There are _______________ Macy's stores all over the world.
3. The store in New York is the _______________ Macy's store.
4. The department store was founded in _______________ .
5. The logo of Macy's is a _______________ .
6. In 1877, there were _______________ stores in New York.
7. Isidor Straus and his wife died when the "Titanic" sank in _______________ .
8. About _______________ people work for Macy's in New York.
9. The tradition of the Thanksgiving Day Parade started in _______________ .
10. The film "Miracle on 34th Street" was first shown in _______________ .
11. The re-make of this film was released in _______________ .

/ 11

II. Are these statements right or wrong?

| | right | wrong |
|---|---|---|
| 1. Saks Fifth Avenue is even bigger than Macy's. | ● | ● |
| 2. The business was founded in 1867. | ● | ● |
| 3. The store is located south of Rockefeller Center. | ● | ● |

/ 3

III. Tick off the correct statement.

1. People go to Tiffany's to buy ● diamonds or rings. – ● skirts or trousers.
2. Tiffany's is located ● near Broadway. – ● on 5th Avenue.
3. The business was founded ● in 1837. – ● in 1873.
4. On the first day Tiffany's only made ● about 50 dollars. – ● about 5 dollars.
5. Many women ● have breakfast at Tiffany's. – ● love "Breakfast at Tiffany's".
6. Tiffany's was also famous for the blue boxes ● which were very expensive. – ● which you got when you bought something.

/ 6

## 2 Vocabulary: Christmas shopping

Find the missing words. The letters of each word are given in brackets.

When you go shopping in New York …

1. you'll see _______________ decorations. (AAEGILNPP)
2. you can buy _______________ things as well as cheap ones. (CEIOPRSU)
3. you'll be amazed by the people – the stores will be _______________ . (CDDEORW)
4. you'll _______________ find everything you want. (AEELLNTUVY)
5. you'll hope to see unusual things – your _______________ will be high. (ACEEINOPSTTX)
6. you might get _______________ up with all the people. (DEF)
7. you might find the _______________ of the Christmas decorations very funny. (CCENOPST)
8. you'll have to _______________________ (2 words!) for hours to see everything. (AADKLNORUW)
9. you'll find that all your bags will _______________ something in the end. (ACINNOT)
10. you'll be happy to _______________ a cup of tea after your shopping tour! (AEIRS)

10

## 3 Vocabulary: American or British English?

Complete the sentences.
When Sinead and Catriona went shopping in New York, Sinead told her cousin what to say in American English.

1. Don't ask for a taxi – ask for a_______________!
2. When you are hungry, you shouldn't order chips, but_______________.
3. And if you want something sweet, don't eat biscuits – eat_______________.
4. I won't call you on your mobile phone – I'll call you on your_______________.
5. And later we'll meet in our_______________, not in our flat.

5

## 4 Grammar: gerund constructions

Fill in the verbs in the correct form. Add the preposition where necessary.

1. When Catriona went shopping with Sinead, she was very interested _______________ (go) to the most famous stores in New York.
2. They thought _______________ (visit) Macy's first.

3. And they weren't bothered about _______________ (spend) all their money.

4. Unfortunately they forgot _______________ (take) more money with them.

5. So they weren't able to stop _______________ (drink) a cup of hot chocolate after their trip.

5

## 5 Grammar: questions

On their way through New York Catriona asked a lot of questions.
Complete the questions by writing down the question tag.

1. We can go to Central Park later, _______________ ?

2. Your friends won't be there, _______________ ?

3. Look at those boys over there – they seem very nice, _______________ ?

4. But I can't invite them to join us, _______________ ?

5. You want a cup of tea, _______________ ?

5

## 6 Grammar: comparison of adjectives

Fill in the adjectives in the correct form.

1. For Catriona New York was the ____________________________ (amazing) place in the world.

2. She had never seen _______________ (tall) buildings than there in New York.

3. And everything seemed to be _______________ (good) than at home in Ireland.

4. She even thought that Sinead's friends were _________________ (interesting) than her own friends.

5. Soon she was convinced that nothing could be _______________ (exciting) as a visit to New York!

5

## 7 Text production: online chat (mediation)

Your school is planning an exchange with students from New York.
Your partner will visit you just before Christmas.
In an online chat, he asks you about the Christmas markets in Germany.
You know that there will be one near your home and you want to tell him about it.

Write this part of the online chat (about 150 words).
Use the information given on the next page.

# Großer Weihnachtsmarkt!

## 8.–24. Dezember

## Marktplatz

mit
➡ vielen Glühweinbuden
➡ einer lebensgroßen Krippe mit echten Schafen
➡ großen Bastelaktionen für die Kleinen (6–7 Jahre)
➡ vielen Buden mit Weihnachtsschmuck
➡ Live-Musik des Weihnachts-Orchesters
➡ Besuch des Nikolaus jeden Sonntag Nachmittag
➡ echten Engeln, die großartige Preise verlosen
und vielen Attraktionen mehr!

Jeden Tag geöffnet
von 10.00 – 19.00 Uhr

___ / 30

___ / 80 Gesamtpunkte 80 – 65 Punkte: ☺ 64 – 41 Punkte: 😐 40 – 0 Punkte: ☹

## Working with words

### 1 German – English

Find the English words. Use the parts of the words given in the box below.

able • ac • as • cept • con • con • de • de • dence • di • duc • ible • in • in • in • ir • ous • out • pen • rage • rate • re • si • spons • sume • tion • tion • tro • un

1. annehmen: ________________
2. Unabhängigkeit: ________________
3. Einleitung, Vorstellung: ________________
4. rücksichtslos: ________________
5. inakzeptabel: ________________
6. Zustand, Bedingung: ________________
7. empörend, unerhört: ________________
8. unverantwortlich: ________________

## Grammar: the infinitive perfect, conditional clauses and more

### 2 The infinitive perfect

Fill in the verbs in the infinitive perfect.

**!** Der Infintiv Perfekt zeigt an, dass etwas in der Vergangenheit anders möglich gewesen wäre.
Er wird immer gebildet aus einem Hilfsverb (*would/could/should/might*), *have* und dem *past participle* des Verbs.

During the wilderness therapy, Rachel had some difficulties.
This is what she thought:

1. It's so cold here! I ____________________________ (bring) a pullover.
2. I have no idea how to prepare these potatoes. I ____________________________ (listen) to my mum.
3. Where is north? Our geography teacher ____________________________ (taught) us how to find the directions!

Für die drei Arten von if-Sätzen gilt:

**Typ 1** – Die Bedingung im if-Satz ist möglich, das Geschehen im Hauptsatz kann durchaus eintreten.
→ Im if-Satz steht das Verb im *simple present*, im Hauptsatz steht das *will-future* oder eine Konstruktion mit einem Hilfsverb (z.B. *can*)
*If the weather **is** nice, we **will go hiking**.*

**Typ 2** – Die Bedingung im if-Satz ist zwar möglich, aber sehr unwahrscheinlich. Das Geschehen im Hauptsatz wird wohl nicht eintreten.
→ Im if-Satz steht das Verb im *simple past*, im Hauptsatz wird *would* und der Infinitiv des Verbs verwendet.
*If the weather **was** nice, we **would go hiking**. But it's raining right now.*

**Typ 3** – Die Bedingung im if-Satz liegt in der Vergangenheit und ist daher unmöglich.
→ Im if-Satz steht das Verb im *past perfect*, im Hauptsatz wird *would* und das Perfekt des Infinitivs (*have* + *past participle*) verwendet.
*If the weather **had been** nice yesterday, we **would have gone hiking**. But it was raining all day long.*

## 3 Conditional clauses

Fill in the verbs in the correct form.

1. If Rachel hadn't taken part in the wilderness therapy, she ____________________ (not – meet) Robert.
2. They would know each other, if they both ____________________ (come) from the same town.
3. Robert will visit her, if Rachel ____________________ (stay) in Colorado this year, too.
4. If they ____________________ (live) in the same town, they would be able to meet every day.
5. If they ________________________ (not be) alone in the wilderness, they wouldn't have learned how to cope with their problems.
6. If Robert finds a job in summer, he ____________________ (invite) Rachel for a weekend.

## 4 Adverbs of degree

Change the given adjectives into adverbs. Then rewrite the sentences using the adverbs as adverbs of degree.

Mit Adverbien kannst du eindringlich und anschaulich gestalten. Das ist vor allem wichtig, wenn du selbst Texte verfasst, zum Beispiel einen Artikel für eine Zeitschrift.

1. (terrible) After a wilderness therapy many teenagers feel sorry about their life. ____________________

   ________________________________________________

2. (**extreme**) When they have to spend one night alone in the wilderness, they are frightened. ____________

____________

3. (**really**) But after the therapy most of them try hard to finish school and find a job. ____________

____________

## 5 The infinitive after question words

Rewrite the following sentences using the infinitive after the question word.

Ein Nebensatz mit Fragewort kann nur dann mithilfe eines Infinitivs gekürzt werden, wenn die Subjekte von Haupt- und Nebensatz identisch sind.

1. Rachel didn't know where she would stay during the wilderness therapy. ____________

____________

____________

2. The guides always wonder what they should tell the teenagers about their stay in the wilderness.

____________

____________

3. James wasn't sure how he should put up his tent. ____________

____________

Rewrite the following sentences using a subordinate clause with question word.

4. James wondered where to put his clothes.

____________

____________

5. The teenagers' parents always wonder what to say to their children when they meet again after the camp.

____________

____________

6. After the camp, the teenagers usually don't ask how to cope with difficulties at school.

____________

____________

Bei den sogenannten ***stative verbs*** findet keine Handlung statt.
Manche Verben können sowohl wie *stative verbs* als auch wie *dynamic verbs* verwendet werden. Dann verändert sich aber die Bedeutung!

*I think Colorado is beautiful.* → Meinung: *stative verb* (Ich glaube ...)
*I'm thinking about visiting Colorado.* → Handlung: *dynamic verb* (Ich überlege gerade ...)

## 6 Stative verbs

Circle the correct form.

This is what James said after the camp:

I **hated/was hating** my life at school. – In the camp everything **seemed/was seeming** different. – One night we **saw/were seeing** a bear, when we **sat/were sitting** around the campfire. – I **think/am thinking** the camp is a great opportunity for teenagers with difficulties. – I **think/am thinking** about going back next year!

# Listening/reading/text production

## 7 Dylan's experiences

Circle the correct word or expression.

When Dylan was 12, he felt **lonely/bored** at school, so he didn't go there any more. – At that time he started **drinking alcohol/taking drugs**. – When he was 14, he ran away and lived **in the streets/in a park**. – When he ran out of money, he even **stole things/begged in the streets**. – When he thinks of that time today, he remembers **every day/nearly nothing**. – His parents sent him to a wilderness therapy, because they felt **frustrated/helpless**. – At first Dylan thought that **he wouldn't survive/he would learn how to cope**. – When he came back from the therapy, he felt **much stronger/more relaxed** than before. – He still wonders if he **will be able to cope with all his problems/will go back to the camp again**.

## 8 The Rocky Mountain Wilderness Therapy

**The Rocky Mountain Youth Program**
Drugs, alcohol, crimes, trouble with the law – many teenagers today try to solve their problems in ways which are not healthy and which lead nowhere. And many parents don't know what to do.
Do you have a teenager who feels lost and who doesn't listen to you any more? Then you should consider our program of wilderness therapy.
Our program is aimed at young people aged 14 to 16. Most of them come from bigger cities and have never experienced nature.

In groups of 8 to 10 members they learn how to cope with any kind of difficulty. They will have to face different challenges alone and together with others, and they have to organize their everyday life in the beautiful Rocky Mountain National Park. While they stay here, they put up and share tents, they prepare their own food and learn how to protect it from bears. They go hiking every day and learn how to use their own abilities. And they cooperate in order to cope with the challenges in the wilderness.
Every evening there are meetings with the therapists in the groups. If necessary, the teenagers can also talk to the therapists in private. At the end of the three-week therapy, the teenagers will stay in the forest alone for three days – only with a tent, some bread, some water, a signal lamp – and a pencil and a notebook.
Because the program is not easy at first for many of the teenagers, they are supported by a team of nurses, rangers, social workers and therapists, so in the end they will have learned how to stick to rules and how to cooperate with other people – and how to cope with the challenges of their own life.
Although the program seems quite expensive at first sight with 450 $ a week, you might be supported by your local social workers. And your children should be worth it!

Tick off the correct boxes.

1. The program is aimed at young people who have problems with
   - school - drugs - friends - their parents - the police - alcohol
2. These young people usually are
   - teenagers - from the countryside - lost in a city - passionate hikers - about 12 years old
3. At the camp they have to
   - work together - be able to cope with challenges on their own - cook - put up tents
   - talk to the therapists in private every day - learn how to protect themselves from wild animals
   - walk every day
4. When they are alone in the wilderness, they take with them:
   - something to eat and drink - something to wear - something to read
   - something to call for help
5. At the camp the teenagers are supported by
   - people with experience in medical support - people with experience in therapies
   - people with experience in teaching young people
   - their parents - people who know how to cope with challenges in nature

## 9 Magazine page

Write a short article about James's Wilderness Therapy for an American magazine (about 150 words). Use your exercise book. Use the information given in his blog on p. 81 (textbook) and the pictures given below.

Wie ein **Zeitungsartikel** sollte auch ein **Artikel für ein Magazin** nicht lang, aber spannend und lebendig geschrieben sein.
Stelle dir also folgende Fragen:

- Habe ich eine packende, knackige Überschrift gefunden?
- Habe ich den Text in Absätze eingeteilt?
- Ist der erste Absatz interessant genug, um den Leser zum Weiterlesen zu verlocken?
- Habe ich persönliche Eindrücke oder Ansichten einbezogen?
- Habe ich die vorhandenen Informationen verwendet und mit eigenen Ideen ergänzt?
- Habe ich die Informationen dadurch lebendig wiedergegeben, dass ich Bilder oder Ereignisse beschreibe, Beispiele nenne, eine Geschichte mit einer unerwarteten Wendung erzähle, Betroffene oder Experten zitiere oder über die Hintergründe spekuliere?
- Ist der Artikel sprachlich richtig verfasst?

Gehe dazu auch die Leitfragen im Vorwort (S. 8) durch.

## 10 Letter to the editor

James's blog entry was published in a newspaper. Write a letter to the editor about wilderness therapies in general (about 150 words). Use your textbook.

Ein **Leserbrief** antwortet in der Regel auf einen Artikel in einer Zeitung oder Zeitschrift und stellt eine **Position** begründet dar. Stelle dir also folgende Fragen:

- Habe ich die passende Anrede (Sir/Madam...) und Einleitung gewählt?
- Wird im ersten Abschnitt deutlich, auf welchen Artikel und welche Aussage ich antworte?
- Wird im ersten Abschnitt außerdem deutlich, weshalb ich den Brief schreibe?
- Erläutere ich meine Gründe für meine Meinung?
- Wird meine Meinung deutlich?
- Endet der Leserbrief mit einer klaren Aussage und meiner Unterschrift?
- Habe ich einen unpersönlichen, formellen Ton gewählt?
- Ist der Leserbrief sprachlich richtig verfasst?

Gehe dazu auch die Leitfragen im Vorwort (S. 8) durch.

Zeit: 45 min Beginn Ende

# Going wild– Test 1

## 1 Listening comprehension: The Black Canyon of the Gunnison Park

I. Circle the correct word or expression.

1. Marty always/sometimes works together with other rangers.
2. Knowing that there are always other people not too far away/Being on his own is something he really likes about his job.
3. The canyons of the National Park are sunny/steep.
4. Parents should keep an eye on their children/hold onto their children when they walk along the canyons.

4

II. Tick off all the things you should do to cope with the bears.

You should...

- know the rules. ● visit the camps. ● take care of your food.
- have a black box with you. ● find a locker for your food.
- eat up everything. ● put your tobacco into a locker.
- not leave any toothpaste lying around in the camp.
- put all things that smell into your tent. ● tidy up after dinner.
- throw away all the food which you have not eaten.

7

III. The campsites – fill in the missing information.

| campsite | sites | electricity – yes/no? | booking – yes/no |
|---|---|---|---|
| South | | | |
| North/East | | | |

6

IV. Fill in the missing words.

1. Most people stay in the National Park only for one or two days, but there are also ______________________ who stay there for some weeks.
2. Hikers should behave in a responsible way towards ______________________: they should, for example, shut the gates in the fences.
3. People should not be ______________________ when they see a snake.

3

## 2 Vocabulary: teenagers' problems

Fill in the missing words.
The teenagers who take part in wilderness therapies have many problems.

1. Some teenagers are ______________________ because their boyfriend or girlfriend has left them.
2. Some teenagers can't stop taking drugs – they are ______________________ to drugs.
3. Some teenagers have problems with the other kids at school. They ______________________ from bullying.
4. Some teenagers only know kids who are not good for them. They ______________________ with the wrong friends.
5. Some teenagers can't talk to their parents any more. They always have ______________________ with their parents.
6. Some teenagers just run away. They pack everything they ______________________ into a bag and leave the house.
7. Some teenagers can't cope with the challenges of everyday life. When their clothes are dirty, they don't even know how to do ______________________ .
8. What they all have in common is that they can't cope with life's challenges – they can't ______________________ with problems.

| |
|---|
| 8 |

## 3 Grammar: the perfect infintive

Fill in the forms of the perfect infinitive.
When the Millers came back from their hike through the National Park, they saw that a bear had visited the camp. This is what they thought:

1. "Out tent is completely destroyed! We shouldn't ______________________ (leave) the food in there!"
2. "Look at that plastic bag – the bear must ______________________ (carry) it around!"
3. "Do you see the scratches on the lockers over there? The bear must ______________________ (try) to open them!"

| |
|---|
| 3 |

## 4 Grammar: the conditional

Fill in the verbs in the correct form.

1. If the parents aren't careful during hikes with their children, there might ____________________ (be) bad accidents.
2. Last year a child was hurt badly when it fell down a slope. This ____________________ (not – happen) if the parents had held onto the child.
3. If there ____________________ (be) more irresponsible parents like that, there would be many more accidents in the National Park.
4. Ranger Marty will help if the parents ____________________ (ask) for advice.
5. He wouldn't have become a ranger if he ____________________ (not – spend) a lot of time in the National Park himself when he was a child.
6. But he wouldn't be happy if the number of wilderness therapies ____________________ (become) more numerous.
7. If too many teenagers with problems ran around in the National Park, he ____________________ (look) for some other job.
8. But even if he____________________ (not – work) as a ranger, he would look for an outdoor job!

8

## 5 Grammar: adverbs of degree

Rewrite the sentences using adverbs of degree.
Find the correct form.

1. (**extreme**) If you meet a bear in the National Park, you must be careful.

____________________________________________

2. (**absolute**) Don't run away. Just move slowly!

____________________________________________

3. (**serious**) If you are attacked by a bear, you can be injured.

____________________________________________

3

## 6 Grammar: the infinitive after question words

Rewrite the following sentences using the infinitive or using a subordinate clause with question word.

1. (**infinitive**) Many tourists don't know where they can get information about the trails through the National Park.

   ____________________

2. (**subordinate clause**) So they wonder where to find the important rules of behaviour for the National Park.

   ____________________

3. (**subordinate clause**) If something happens, they often don't know who to ask for help.

   ____________________

4. (**infinitive**) But the rangers usually know how they can find the hikers after an accident.

   ____________________

4

## 7 Grammar: stative verbs

Fill in the verb in the correct tense, simple or progressive form.

When Ranger Marty came home from work, he told his wife:

1. "Today I heard about an accident. It ____________ (sound) awful!
2. ____________ (you – think) that so many tourists will come again tomorrow?
3. When I ____________ (walk) along the canyon, I saw at least ten groups of teenagers.
4. I ____________ (hate) it when there are so many people around!

4

## 8 Text production: article for a magazine (mediation)

Write a short article about the National Park "Bayerischer Wald" for an American magazine (about 150 words).
Use the pictures and the background information given on the right page.
Use your exercise book.

Bayerischer Wald

**1.**
- im Osten Bayerns, direkt an der Grenze zu Tschechien
- gegründet am 7. Oktober 1970 als erster Nationalpark Deutschlands – erweitert 1997
- Größe: 24.250 Hektar – größte Waldfläche Mitteleuropas
- berühmte Berge: Lusen, Großer Rachel, Großer Falkenstein
- über 700.000 Besucher pro Jahr

**2.**
- mehr als 200 km Radwege, allerdings viele Bergstrecken
- zu berühmten Sehenswürdigkeiten nur Wanderwege
- kleine Raststellen mit Fahrradhaltebügeln
- E-Bikes erlaubt (wie normale Fahrräder)
- Reiten nur auf gekennzeichneten Wegen erlaubt

**3.**
- Wildniscamp: für Gruppen (Schulklassen, Familien, Vereine) zu bestimmten Themen (z. B. Klimawandel)
- betreut durch Sozialpädagogen
- für jeweils eine Woche buchbar
- Kosten: 400 € pro Person /pro Woche

/ 30

80 – 65 Punkte: ☺ 64 – 41 Punkte: 😐 40 – 0 Punkte: ☹ Gesamtpunkte / 80

Zeit: 45 min Beginn Ende

# Protecting the environment – Test 2

## 1 Reading comprehension: protest against fracking

"No Fracking Here!"

When the town council of Longfield in Osage County, Colorado, announced that a new fracking site would be opened next year near the town, the reactions weren't all positive.
"We need the fracking site", the spokesman of the town council said. It will bring a lot of jobs which are needed in the little town with many farmers. And it will bring a lot of money. He added: "Just think of all the oil which is waiting underground to be pumped up! It would be a waste of resources not to open the site!"
There were, however, voices who didn't agree with the plans. In the meantime, a protest group has been organized by Carl Johnson, a farmer from Longfield. "We have talked to the town council, but they won't listen to us. We want to be taken seriously! They are going to destroy our land, our farms and then even our lives!" Johnson is joined by 20 members of the Longfield community who all have fears and worries about this new site. They are convinced that the dangers of fracking are far too serious to be risked. As Johnson puts it: "Everybody knows that fracking is a real threat to the environment and the people. The toxic chemicals can pollute the water we drink, the water we give to our animals and which we use for our fields." And not only the water may be polluted. In some other towns the air has even become yellow, because gas has been led into the air which people and animals breathe in. And there have even been accidents, when gas came out of the tap and houses were blown up.
And that's not all: Johnson has heard about another danger. Sometimes the water which is used for drilling leaks or is even led into the fields around the drilling sites, and this water is often mixed with salt. "If our fields are contaminated with salt, we will never be able to keep our ranches. There is no way to clean the fields again!" And in this respect he seems to be right: there are methods to clean ground which is polluted by chemicals, but nobody has ever invented a method to clean ground which is polluted by salt. The salt will cause every plant to die, and then nothing will grow for years to come.
Johnson talks about his cousin, who lives near a fracking site. When a pipeline broke five years ago, thousands of liters of salt water leaked out into his fields. "And today there aren't any trees, any bushes nor grass. All his fields look dry and sandy now. His ranch is completely ruined."
The new protest group wants to stop the town council's plans now. They are going to demonstrate first. And they will put up posters in every store and public building in the community. Johnson says: "People have to find out about the dangers. The town council hasn't taken the problem seriously enough!" If all this doesn't help, Johnson and his group have even bigger plans. They are going to block the roads, they are going stop the machines and the workers. And they are planning to tell the national media about their worries.
The town council has already announced that no such activities will be allowed. "We need the money and the jobs which the new drilling site will bring", says Martin McGregor, head of the town council. "The inhabitants of Longfield are afraid of the new drilling methods, of course. But people are always afraid of new things. Besides, the dangers of fracking are exaggerated and should simply be ignored."

Carl Johnson is really angry about statements like these. "There have been many accidents already, and there are scientists who talk about the dangers. So we can't just ignore the risks. And if an accident happens here, it will be too late! We will all lose our ranches."

I. Fill in the missing words!

The town council of Longfield is convinced that the new fracking site is needed because it will bring (1)____________________ and (2)____________________ to the little community with many farms. Moreover, not drilling for oil would be a (3)____________________________________ . The protest group, however, want the town council to (4)____________________ to them. They are afraid that in the end the fracking site will cause a lot of damage to (5)____________________ and to (6)____________________, so that in the end their (7)____________________ will be destroyed. – They want to talk about the dangers of fracking – the (8)____________________ and the (9)____________________ might be polluted by the chemicals, which is bad for both the (10)____________________ and the (11)____________________ . Moreover, there might be accidents caused by leaking (12)____________________ . And if water mixed with salt is led into the fields, the ground will be (13)____________________ forever. 13

II. Tick off the activities the protest group are planning!

- organizing demonstrations
- taking part in meetings with the politicians
- talking to the media
- destroying the machines
- preventing the trucks from driving to the site
- using violence against the company's bosses

3

III. Complete the sentences. Write into your exercise book.

1. The town council is against the protest, so they will ...
2. Martin McGregor still thinks that the site is needed, although he ...
3. Martin McGregor knows that there are dangers, but he thinks they should ...
4. Carl Johnson is angry, because there have already been accidents and still the town council ...

4

## 2 Vocabulary: protecting the environment

Fill in the missing words.

When a new fracking site is planned, many people hope to make a profit, so they are (1)____________________ of the plans. But there are also others who think that the sites are not safe enough – they (2)____________________ that the sites are safe enough. When these people want to protest and do something against the plans, they often join an (3)____________________ . They are often afraid that the (4)____________________ which all people and animals need to drink might be (5)____________________ if an accident happens at the site and (6)____________________ chemicals are led into the ground. They also fear that the gas which is (7)____________________ from the ground might cause damage, too. But in most cases their petitions and letters and questions and protests are (8)____________________ by the town councils.

___ / 8

## 3 Grammar: the perfect infintive

Fill in the verb in the perfect infinitive.

After the accident on the fracking site near the farm of John's cousin they knew better:

1. "We should ____________________ (organize) more demonstrations!"
2. "The politicians should ____________________ (listen) to us!"
3. "The company must ____________________ (know) that there were problems!"

___ / 3

## 4 Grammar: the conditional

Fill in the verb in the correct form.

Carl Johnson from Longfield is a member of the protest group against the new fracking site. He says:

1. "If we ____________________ (not protest), the companies will build new sites everywhere!"
2. "Last week we even blocked the road. If the police hadn't come, we ____________________ (stay) there for some days."
3. "Our grandfathers ______________________________ (would be) disappointed, if we hadn't done anything against the site!"

4. "And if the town council doesn't stop the plans, we ______________________ (even – take) more action!"

5. "If there ______________________ (be) more activists, we would be more successful."

6. "But there are still people who don't take the risks of fracking seriously. And if there ______________________ (be) an accident, they will be very sorry."

7. "And then they will say: if we ______________________ (know) this before, we would have taken action, too."

8. "But then it will be too late for all of us – if there's an accident at the fracking site, all our fields ______________________ (destroy – *passive*!)."

___ / 8

## 5 Grammar: adverbs of degree

Rewrite the sentences using adverbs of degree! Find the correct form.

1. (high) The fracking companies say that the risks of fracking are exaggerated.

_______________________________________________

2. (dangerous) Protest groups, however, think that it would be wrong not to take the risks seriously.

_______________________________________________

3. (extreme) The movie "Gasland" shows that the risks are high.

_______________________________________________

___ / 3

## 6 Grammar: the infinitive after question words

Rewrite the following questions using the infinitive OR using a subordinate clause with question word.

1. (infinitive) When Carl Johnson decided to join the protest group, he didn't know at first where he could meet the others. ______________________________

_______________________________________________.

2. (subordinate clause) The other members of the group asked him what to write onto the posters.

_______________________________________________

_______________________________________________

3. (**subordinate clause**) And they asked him what to bring for the next meeting.

______________________________________________

______________________________________________

4. (**infinitive**) Soon Carl Johnson found out how he could organize everything.

______________________________________________

______________________________________________

4

## 7 Grammar: stative verbs

Fill in the verb in the correct tense, simple or progressive form.

1. On the way to the demonstration, Carl Johnson was walking next to his friend Charlie.

   He ____________________ (like) him a lot.

2. Charlie ____________________ (also – think) that fracking is too dangerous.
3. He ____________________ (think) about joining Carl's protest group at the moment.
4. Carl is very happy about this – when they ____________________ (block) the road last week,

   the police came. They could have needed more people!

4

## 8 Text production: letter to the editor

You have read an article about a new fracking site in the fields near Longfield in Osage County, Colorado. You have read that there is a group of inhabitants who are protesting against these plans by putting up posters and if necessary, even by taking action. They want to block the roads, for example.
Write a letter to the editor of the local newspaper about the fracking plans and the plans of the protest group (about 150 words).
Use your exercise book.

30

80 Gesamtpunkte 80 – 65 Punkte: ☺ 64 – 41 Punkte: 😐 40 – 0 Punkte: ☹

## Working with words

### 1 Jumbled Letters

Find the word by bringing the letters into the correct order.

1. Wettbewerb: (cenostt) ____________________
2. herzzerreißend: (aabeeghiknrrt) ____________________
3. Dokumentation: (adekmnortuy) ____________________
4. verlegen: (ccefilnoosssu-) ____________________
5. gefährden: (adeeijoprz) ____________________
6. reich: (aehltwy) ____________________

## Grammar: adjectives/adverbs and infinitive

!

Adjektive beschreiben immer, wie etwas IST (= einen Zustand).
Adverben beschreiben immer, wie etwas GETAN wird (= ein Prozess, eine Handlung) – mit einer Ausnahme: **Wenn ein anderes Adjektiv beschrieben wird, wird ebenfalls das Adverb gebildet**.
Deshalb wird nach Verben der Wahrnehmung (*look, sound*), des Eindrucks (*seem, feel*) und der Meinung (*consider, call*) ein Adjektiv verwendet, das den Zustand des Wahrgenommenen bzw. Beschriebenen darstellt.

### 2 Adjectives and adverbs

Fill in the adjective or adverb.

1. When Carmen came to America, she felt ____________________ (lonely).
2. She tried to find a job ____________________ (quick).
3. She still considered her family ____________________ (important).
4. At last she was offered a job which sounded ____________________ (fantastic).
5. She felt ____________________ (real) ____________________ (happy) when she heard of her children.

!

Der **Infinitiv** wird **ohne *to*** verwendet,
- wenn er nach *make* oder *let* steht oder
- wenn er nach einem Verb der Wahrnehmung (*see*, *hear*) steht.

## 3 The infinitive without *to*

Fill in the verb in the infinitive with or without *to*.

1. At first Carmen's children didn't let her ____________________ (go).
2. They wanted her ____________________ (stay) with them.
3. It was very hard for Carmen to listen to her children ____________________ (cry).
4. This made her ____________________ (cry), too.
5. But she was supposed ____________________ (leave), so she packed her things and tried

   ____________________ (find) a better life for her whole family.

# Reading/listening

## 4 Silicon Valley

Located near San Francisco, Sillicon Valley has become the most important center of IT and HichTech industries worldwide. Some decades ago, Sunnyvale was just an ordinary place near a university, but when in 1951 the industrial area was founded near the famous Stanford University, the development of this area started. At first there were only small businesses there, but when in the 1960s and 1970s computer technologies became more and more important, the IT industry grew and grew – until in 1971 the name "Silicon Valley" was coined for this place. Today the name is even copied for centers of IT industries worldwide, and many American and international companies have their seats in California. Everybody knows the names: Google, Amazon, Facebook, Hewlett-Packard, but also Siemens or Nokia have offices there.
This center of computer technologies also brought some negative consequences for the area. Many toxic chemicals are needed for the production of computers. Everybody was shocked when in 1981 people found out that some of the old tanks for these chemicals had leaked so that vast areas of Silicon Valley are still polluted. Some of the companies with polluted ground have been given up, so the government will have to clean the ground. But some of the companies are still there in Silicon Valley – and they are doing what they have always done: they are inventing new methods and techniques. Some companies have invested a lot of money to develop new methods of cleaning those highly toxic and polluted grounds. And these methods can be used in other areas in the world as well – the investment seems to have been worth it.

I. Complete the sentences.

1. Silicon Valley is located in __________________ .
2. Before 1951, the place where Silicon Valley is located was called __________________ .
3. At first the area was used only as an __________________________________ .
4. In the 1960s and 1970s there were more and more businesses there which worked on __________________________________.
5. Silicon Valley is not only a center for American companies, but also for __________________ companies.
6. After 1980 some spots were found where __________________ had polluted the ground.
7. Some companies are still there, and they are developing new methods of _________________________ .
8. The development of new technologies is exactly what the companies in Silicon Valley __________________ .

## 5 The actress

Right or wrong?

| | | right | wrong |
|---|---|---|---|
| 1. | The girl is 24 now. | ○ | ○ |
| 2. | She has wanted to become an actress when she finished school. | ○ | ○ |
| 3. | She comes from a town near Los Angeles. | ○ | ○ |
| 4. | Her parents wanted her to stay with them. | ○ | ○ |
| 5. | She doesn't earn enough money to get along as an actress. | ○ | ○ |
| 6. | For her, it's difficult to get a job as an actress, because she is too old. | ○ | ○ |
| 7. | It's important to attend acting classes. | ○ | ○ |
| 8. | She wants to go back, although she is afraid of her friends' reaction. | ○ | ○ |
| 9. | She will stay in Los Angeles because she has found the chance to perform on stage. | ○ | ○ |

## Text production

### 6 Cartoon

Describe the cartoon and explain its message.

Wenn du einen Cartoon analysieren sollst, gehst du am besten nach folgenden Schritten vor:

- Erst nennst du das Thema des Cartoons.
- Dann beschreibst du die wesentlichen Elemente.
- Anschließend stellst du den Cartoon in den Zusammenhang, in dem er zu verstehen ist.
- Abschließend nennst du die Aussage des Cartoons bzw. die Kritik, die geübt wird.

Stelle dir also folgende Fragen:

- Habe ich den Cartoon verstanden und das Thema bzw. die Aussage erkannt?
- Habe ich den Text in Absätze eingeteilt?
- Habe ich den Cartoon sinnvoll beschrieben?
- Habe ich die Informationen sinnvoll erklärt?
- Ist der Text sprachlich richtig verfasst?

Gehe dazu auch die Leitfragen im Vorwort (S. 8) durch.

## 7 Comment

You have read that in Los Angeles an group of people want to establish a center for Hispanic immigrants who are treated very badly. Write a comment about these plans (about 150 words). Use your exercise book.

Wie bei einem Leserbrief geht es beim *comment* darum, dass du deine Meinung begründet darstellst.
Stelle dir deshalb folgende Fragen:

- Habe ich im ersten Absatz das Thema genannt?
- Habe ich sinnvoll Gründe für meine Meinung gefunden und diese dann genügend erklärt und belegt?
- Habe ich mit meinem schwächsten Grund begonnen und den stärksten ans Ende gesetzt?
- Wird am Ende des *comment* meine Meinung noch einmal genannt?
- Ist der *comment* sprachlich richtig verfasst?

Gehe dazu auch die Leitfragen im Vorwort (S. 8) durch.

Zeit: 45 min Beginn Ende

# Hispanics in California – Test 1

## 1 Listening comprehension: Miguel

I. Tick off the correct box.

1. Miguel was born ● in California. ● in Spain. ● in Mexico.
2. His whole family speak Spanish ● only sometimes. ● quite often. ● a little bit.
3. His father was born ● in Spain. ● in California. ● in Mexico.
4. Miguel's father came to California ● with his mother.
   ● with his mother and his brothers and sisters. ● on his own.
5. Miguel's grandmother left home because ● she wanted to make money.
   ● she wanted a better life for her children. ● she liked California.
6. When Miguel's father arrived in California, he ● was only ten years old.
   ● he was a teenager. ● he stayed there for 10 years.
7. In California Miguel's father had the chance ● to go to school.
   ● to get a job. ● to earn some money on his own.

7

II. Complete the text.

After their arrival in the USA his mother found a job on a (1)__________________ . The job was very (2)__________________ and the children had to (3)__________________ their mother in summer. There was no limit to the (4)__________________ , and in summer the weather was often very (5)__________________ . They had to collect strawberries in little (6)__________________ , and they only got two dollars for one. Miguel's father (7)__________________ the job.

7

III. Right or Wrong?

| | | right | wrong |
|---|---|---|---|
| 1. | Later Miguel's father was lucky and found a good job in a restaurant. | ● | ● |
| 2. | The people there treated him very badly. | ● | ● |
| 3. | He learned at home and was able to go to university. | ● | ● |
| 4. | His wife's family liked him a lot. | ● | ● |
| 5. | Miguel's father thinks that family life in Mexico is closer than in California. | ● | ● |
| 6. | He thinks that it's always a good idea to start a new life in the US if you come from Mexico. | ● | ● |

6

## 2 Vocabulary: Hispanics in California

Complete the sentences with the most appropriate word from the box below.

**shy • relieved • enter • rehearse • encouraged • jeopardize • mountains • read • violated • border • fences • self-conscious • apart • keep up • income • ruin**

1. Miguel's father crossed the __________________ near San Diego.
2. He had to climb over some high __________________ at night, which was very dangerous.
3. When his mother tried to find a job, she always felt very __________________. All the other seemed to know so much more than her!
4. It wasn't easy for her to talk to people, because she had always been a very __________________ person.
5. At least she had her children with her. She couldn't have lived __________________ from her family!
6. And she wanted to __________________ her old traditions.
7. When she finally found a job, her __________________ was not very high.
8. And she often felt that her rights were __________________ .
9. She kept on working, because she didn't want to __________________ her family.
10. But after some years she told everybody in Mexico not to __________________ California.

10

## 3 Grammar: adjectives and adverbs

Fill in the adjective or adverb.

1. For many immigrants life in Mexico seemed __________________ (relaxed).
2. They remember meeting their friends in the streets and listening to them __________________ (talk) about their families.
3. This seems __________________ (different) to them in California.
4. Miguel's father was convinced that the Americans considered their jobs __________________ (high/comparison!) than their families.

5. So he felt __________________ (extreme) __________________ (disappointed) when he started his new life in California.

6. The thought of Mexico made him __________________ (sad).

8 7. But then he went out again and tried to work as __________________ (hard) as possible.

## 4 Grammar: the infinitive with and without *to*

Fill in the verb with or without *to*.

1. Miguel's wife made him __________________ (talk) English instead of Spanish.
2. They let their children __________________ (speak) Spanish at home.
3. But they expect them __________________ (use) the English language in public.
4. They make their son __________________ (work) very hard for school.
5. He is supposed __________________ (go) to a college next year.
6. But on Saturday they let him __________ (go) out with his friends.

6

## 5 Grammar: mixed tenses

Fill in the verbs in the correct form.

Before she met Miguel, Jenny (1)__________________ (not – know) any Hispanic people. If she (2)__________________ (meet) him some years later, her family might (3)__________________ (reacted) in a different way. But Miguel tried not to get angry when Jenny's mother behaved in a very unfriendly way. Since that time he (4)__________________ (learn) that as a Hispanic you must behave in a very polite way, so that the others (5)__________________ (not – talk) badly about you. And he (6)__________________ (tell) his children about his experiences!

6

## 6 Text production: cartoon

Describe the cartoon and explain its message.
Write about 150 words.

*Thank God the government is finally doing something against all these immigrants. They are taking all our jobs away!*

| | |
|---|---|
| | 30 |

80 – 65 Punkte: ☺ 64 – 41 Punkte: 😐 40 – 0 Punkte: ☹ Gesamtpunkte | 80

Zeit: 45 min Beginn Ende

## Hollywood – Test 2

### 1 Reading comprehension: child stars now and then

Everybody knows Jody Foster, Leonardo diCaprio or Lindsey Lohan. But who remembers John Hart? He acted in his first film when he was five, and his parents hoped that he might be the next child superstar. But while his first film was quite successful, the second and third films weren't. The silly and superficial stories couldn't attract many people, and his career ended when he was only seven years old.
And still he was lucky. He went back to school and to the life of a "normal teenager" with all the problems. And his parents were disappointed, but they supported him then, too, and didn't make him try to get acting jobs or to get plastic surgery to look better.
But what must it be like for a child to become famous and then be forgotten again all of a sudden?
One actress must have felt this very strongly – she still is one of the most famous and best-known child stars of all times in Hollywood: Shirley Temple.
She was born in 1928 in Santa Monica, California. As soon as she could walk, she wanted to dance, too, so her parents let her take dancing lessons in Los Angeles. At this school she was then discovered by a film director, and she performed in her first film at the age of four. Only two years later she had her breakthrough in the movie business. She danced and acted together with the greatest stars of her time. Fred Astaire and Gary Cooper are only two of her partners. She took part in many films, and all of them were extremely successful. Even the American president at that time, Roosevelt, admitted to be one of her greatest fans.
And she earned a lot of money. In 1937, when she was only 9 years old, she ranked seventh in the list of the people who earned most in the USA.
But these times didn't last too long. When other film companies started to imitate her films, her popularity decreased – by then she was only 12 years old. For ten more years she tried to become a superstar again, but she never found the former fame and success again. So at the age of 22 she put an end to her career as a film star, disappointed, yes, but still wealthy.
From then on she worked for TV stations and even started a political career. She never returned to the show business.
What a difference to child stars today! Most of them – or their parents – can't accept that not every child star will be a superstar as an adult, too. And many of today's child stars will end up addicted to drugs or alcohol, depressed, in trouble with the law, and not being able to lead a normal life.

I. Right or wrong?

| | | right | wrong |
|---|---|---|---|
| 1. | Jody Foster started her career as a child star and she is still very successful. | ● | ● |
| 2. | John Hart was a child star and he is still a popular actor. | ● | ● |
| 3. | His films weren't seen by many people. | ● | ● |
| 4. | He was an actor for more than seven years. | ● | ● |
| 5. | He was luckier than many other child stars. | ● | ● |

| | | right | wrong |
|---|---|---|---|
| 6. | His parents didn't support him after the end of his career. | ● | ● |
| 7. | If parents want their children to be stars, they sometimes make them go to the dentist's to have their teeth whitened. | ● | ● |

7

**II.** Complete the text.

Shirley Temple was one of the most famous child stars in (1)__________________ and she is still known to many people today. She started taking dancing lessons, because she (2)__________________. When a (3)__________________ saw her at the dancing school, he gave her (4)__________________ – and she was only four years old.

When she was (5)__________________, she became famous all around the world, and she performed in films together with the greatest stars of her time. Even the (6)__________________ of the USA was one of her fans.

After some (7)__________________ with the studios, she ended her career as a movie star at the age of 22. She later became a (8)__________________ activist.

8

**III.** Tick off the problems which many child stars of today have:

- depressions
- anorexia
- illegal activities
- addiction to alcohol
- addiction to games
- loneliness
- poverty
- no experience of a "normal life"

5

## 2 Vocabulary: film stars

Complete the sentences. The German translations of the words are given in the box.

> **sich schämen • Beweis • wachsen • Schauspielerei • eitel • „schießen"/(einen Film) drehen • gleichmäßig • proben • schädlich • ermutigen**

1. Everybody is very excited when a new film is being __________________ .
2. The actors usually __________________ their scenes for hours.
3. Some of them are so __________________ that they don't talk to the fans who want to watch.
4. But some are also very nice and __________________ young actors to carry on.

5. The actors are also asked to eat only healthy food – they must avoid everything ________________ .
6. Some of the stars complain about the food at the set – they want to see ________________ that food is healthy.
7. Sometimes even the directors become annoyed with all the ________________ at the set!
8. But with every film the income ________________ .
9. So they aren't even ________________ of bad and stupid films.
10. Everything is fine as long as the money comes in in a ________________ flow!

10

## 3 Grammar: adjectives and adverbs

Fill in the adjective or the adverb.

1. The story of Shirley Temple seems ________________ (sad) at first glance.
2. But she considered her career to be ________________ (wonderful).
3. Of course as a child she felt very ________________ (disappointed) when nobody wanted to see her films any more.
4. So she worked even ________________ (hard/comparison!).
5. This really sounds ________________ (terrible) ________________ (bad) for every child!
6. Later she found a new job. After all, she could talk to people very ________________ (good).
7. So a TV station gave her a job, which made her very ________________ (happy).

8

## 4 Grammar: the infinitive with and without *to*

Fill in the infinitive with or without *to*.

1. Some directors are very strict with the actors. They don't let them ________________ (walk) around the set.
2. And they make them ________________ (eat) special food.
3. They expect the actors ________________ (do) whatever they tell them.
4. But some actors let these directors ________________ (give) them instructions – and then do whatever they want.

5. Things like these usually make directors ____________________ (shout).

6. And sometimes they make the actors ____________________ (leave) the set.

6

## 5 Grammar: mixed tenses

Fill in the verbs in the correct tense.

Before Shirley Temple became a political activist, she (1)____________________ (work) for a TV station. But after a while she found out that only talking to people was not the right thing to do for her. While she (2)____________________ (think) about looking for a different job, a friend of hers (3)____________________ (suggest) to her to become a politician. It is known that she was quite good, and she (4)____________________ (develop) some projects that are still there today. But even after this career she is still seen as the greatest child star of all times. And people (5)______________________ (still – enjoy) her films in the future! If only she (6)____________________ (know) this when she was a child!

6

## 6 Text production: comment

In Germany some people say that girls shouldn't be allowed to take part in beauty pageants when they are younger than 14. Write a comment on this suggestion (about 150 words).

______________________________________________________________________

______________________________________________________________________

______________________________________________________________________

______________________________________________________________________

______________________________________________________________________

______________________________________________________________________

______________________________________________________________________

______________________________________________________________________

______________________________________________________________________

30

80 – 64 Punkte: ☺ 63 – 41 Punkte: 😐 40 – 0 Punkte: ☹ Gesamtpunkte 80

## Working with words

### 1 Finding words

Write down the missing words.

1. only few days ago = ______________________
2. the opposite of the "city center" = ______________________
3. the little garden or place next to the house = ______________________
4. a synonym for "place" = ______________________
5. the time you don't spend working = ______________________
6. a person who belongs to another person = ______________________

### 2 Background knowledge: American history

The words or expressions printed in blue are wrong. Correct them and write down the word(s) in the lines below the statements.

Lies dir vorher S. 136 im Textbuch noch einmal durch.

1. By the 1700s, **America's empire** included colonies in Africa or the Caribbean.

   ______________________________________________

2. When Britain invented new taxes for the colonies, the Americans **were asked first**.

   ______________________________________________

3. When in 1773 a new **tax for coffee** was introduced, the Americans took action.

   ______________________________________________

4. They disguised themselves as **British soldiers** and went on board the British ships.

   ______________________________________________

5. This "party" was the beginning of the **"War of Revolution"**.

   ______________________________________________

## Grammar: relative clauses and the present

### 3 Relative clauses

Connect the sentences by using relative clauses! Write down the complete sentences and tick off "N" for a non-defining relative clause and "D" for a defining relative clause.

> In einem *defining relative clause* beschreibt der Relativsatz ein Wort aus dem Hauptsatz, das ohne den Relativsatz nicht verständlich ist.

1. Denzel's mother works at the museum. The museum shows the history of the African-Americans.

   ● N ● D ____________________

   ____________________

2. Yesterday Denzel went there with Tom. He had met Tom at school.

   ● N ● D ____________________

   ____________________

3. They both like the room best. The room contained some pictures of Martin Luther King.

   ● N ● D ____________________

   ____________________

4. Their history teacher had already told them about this activist. Their history teacher is very nice.

   ● N ● D ____________________

   ____________________

> Folgende Anwendungsmöglichkeiten des *present* kennst du:
>
> Das *present simple* wird verwendet für eine Handlung in der Gegenwart, die regelmäßig stattfindet. Daneben wird damit auch eine Handlung in der Zukunft ausgedrückt, die feststeht (z.B. in einem Fahrplan, in einem Stundenplan etc.).
>
> Das *present progressive* wird verwendet für eine konkrete Handlung in der Gegenwart, die jetzt gerade stattfindet.
> Daneben wird damit auch ein persönliches Vorhaben in der näheren Zukunft ausgedrückt.
>
> Lies zur Verwendung des *will-future* und des *going-to-future* eventuell die Übersicht im Übungsteil des ersten Kapitels durch.

## 4 The present

Fill in the verb in the correct form.

1. Denzel can't visit his mother right now. She ____________________ (guide) a group through the exhibition.
2. He ____________________ (visit) the museum together with his new friend Tom next weekend.
3. That ____________________ (be) very interesting!
4. He says: "I have heard so much about the Civil Rights Movement at school today, so I think I ____________________ (read) a book about it this afternoon."
5. "Maybe I can pick up Mum after work. Her work shift ____________________ (finish) at five o'clock."

## Listening/reading

## 5 The best job in the world

Complete the sentences.

1. David took the job, because when he finished school he ____________________ ____________________.
2. He found the job in ____________________.
3. When he worked as a tester for water slides, he had to ____________________ and test the slides.
4. What he found a bit difficult was that he ____________________ very often.
5. There were many applicants for the job, and he got the job mainly because he ____________________.
6. The money he was paid was ok for him, because he knew he would ____________________.

## 6 The alligator hunter

### Martin Hancock, alligator hunter

When most people go to work in the morning, they take a briefcase with papers with them. Not so Martin Hancock. He takes a gun and a lot of rope with him.
It's eight o'clock in the morning. A lady gets into her car to drive to work. Then there is a strange sound. "Rats? A flat tire?" she thinks – and calls the repair service. But the man says: "No, Ma'am, you don't have any rats in the car nor a flat tire. There's an alligator under your car." And that's the moment when the lady calls Martin Hancock.
In Florida there is plenty of work for him to do. There are about a million alligators in Florida, and they don't have enough places to live. So they try to settle in swimming pools, on golf courses, in garages, in parks – just everywhere. And it's Hancock's job to hunt them.
But it's not only alligators he hunts. He has also comes across pythons and other snakes, mountain lions, zebras or monkeys. Although he is always very careful when he finds an exotic animal, he has already been hurt twice. He is well aware that the question is not if he will be attacked by an animal, but when. But he knows this – and he respects the animals. As he says: "The animals are only following their instincts. When they feel threatened, they'll bite. It's only natural."

Right or Wrong?

| | right | wrong |
|---|---|---|
| 1. Martin Hancock's things he needs for his job are very unusual. | ● | ● |
| 2. One morning he was called because there was a rat in a lady's car. | ● | ● |
| 3. In Florida there is always enough for him to do. | ● | ● |
| 4. The alligators settle in places where there aren't many people. | ● | ● |
| 5. Martin Hancock knows how to hunt other animals, too. | ● | ● |
| 6. He knows that wild animals are very dangerous, but he doesn't care. | ● | ● |
| 7. He understands that the animals only do what they must do when he tries to hunt them. | ● | ● |

## Text production

### 7 A blog entry

When Catriona visited Sinead in New York, they spent one day at Ellis Island.
Write Catriona's blog entry about this day (about 150 words).
Write into your exercise book. Use the information given on p. 62–65 in your textbook.

!

Bei einem Blog werden wie bei einem Tagebuch die persönlichen Erlebnisse geschildert.
Stelle dir deshalb folgende Fragen:

- Habe ich gesagt, worum es geht?
- Habe ich meine Eindrücke beschrieben?
- Habe ich dabei auch meine Gefühle und Gedanken dargestellt?
- Habe ich die Informationen, die ich interessant und spannend finde, einbezogen?
- Ist der Eintrag sprachlich richtig verfasst?

Gehe dazu auch die Leitfragen im Vorwort (S. 8) durch.

## 8 Job application

In your local supermarket you have found the following ad:

We are looking for young people to work as newspaper carriers
for our supermarket paper!

The carriers should be at least 14 years old and reliable.
The newspaper is published on Saturday,
so it should be delivered on Saturday or Sunday.

You can hand in your application at the information desk
inside the supermarket!

Write an application for the job.

Zeit: 45 min Beginn Ende

## Philadelphia– Test 1

### 1 Reading comprehension: the Liberty Bell

**The Liberty Bell**

It was a great day, and one that history would never forget. On the 8th of July, 1776, the streets and parks of Philadelphia were crowded. Everybody wanted to listen to the reading of the new Declaration of Independence. And the ceremony on Independence Square was not just reading the text – the importance of this day was emphasized by the loud and solemn ringing of a huge bell – the Liberty Bell.

The bell had been brought to Philadelphia long before that day. It had been produced in London, but even before it could be installed, the first damages were revealed. Luckily there were some craftsmen who could repair it before hanging it into its place.

Today, the Liberty Bell can still be seen in Philadelphia as part of the Independence National Historic Park, and thousands of people visit it every year. If you want to listen to the bell, however, you will be disappointed. It was in 1846 when it was last heard – on the occasion of George Washington's birthday. It is said that during this event the old damages were revealed again, and since then it has never been repaired again.

Nevertheless it is still the most important symbol of freedom and democracy in the USA, and it has become part of the famous UNESCO world heritage. Moreover, copies of the bell were made and taken to different parts of the world – one copy was taken to Berlin in 1950, to give people there hope for freedom during the times of the Cold War. This Berlin bell was financed by the American people, who donated money to produce the bell. The Berlin bell can still be heard today: it is rung every day at midday, and at midnight on holidays. Moreover, it is rung for special occasions. Thus, it could be heard on October 3, 1990, when Germany was reunited. On September 13, 2001, it was rung for seven minutes, while thousands of Germans were commemorating the victims of the terror attacks on the World Trade Center in New York two days before.

With this close relationship it is clear that different legends and stories about the Germans in Philadelphia have become well-known. One of the most popular legends is the so-called Muehlenberg legend. It says that in the 19th century the Americans carried out a vote in parliament, about the question whether German should be the second official language in the USA. It is said that they nearly decided on German and English as official languages – and then the USA would be a German-speaking country today.

This legend, however, is indeed only a legend. There has never been a vote for English or for German as the one common language. What is true, however, is that a group of German immigrants asked for an official translation of the laws into German in 1794. Their aim was to help the new immigrants from Germany, who hadn't learned the English language yet, to integrate in their new home country. But this petition was refuted – with 42 to 41 votes. The one vote came from the speaker of the parliament, Frederick Muehlenberg, who had German origins himself and who spoke German at home. His opinion was that the Germans should become Americans – the faster the better. No other vote about the language has taken place.

I. Are the statements right or wrong?

| | | right | wrong |
|---|---|---|---|
| 1. | On the 8th of July, 1776, the Declaration of Independence was signed. | ● | ● |
| 2. | Nobody in Philadelphia stayed at home. | ● | ● |
| 3. | The ceremony included the reading of the Declaration of Independence. | ● | ● |
| 4. | The bell had come all the way from Europe. | ● | ● |
| 5. | European workers could repair the bell before July 1776. | ● | ● |
| 6. | The bell is still rung every day in Philadelphia. | ● | ● |
| 7. | The bell was meant as a birthday present for George Washington. | ● | ● |

7

II. Complete the text.

For many Americans, the Liberty Bell shows the importance of (1)______________________ and democracy. The UNESCO has declared it one of the most important (2)______________________ in history. You can see different (3)______________________ of the bell around the world. One Liberty Bell was taken to Berlin from (4)______________________ in 1950 – it was paid for by the (5)______________________ and given to the city of Berlin as a present. It can still be heard, because it is rung (6)______________________ and on special occasions. The inhabitants of Berlin, for example, rang the bell after the (7)______________________ in New York in 2001.

7

III. Circle the correct word or expression

1. There is a very **close/difficult** relationship between Germans and Philadelphia.
2. The so-called Muehlenberg legend refers to the time of the **18th century/19th century**.
3. The American parliament discussed the introduction of **German as the official language/German and English as the two official languages**.
4. Some German immigrants indeed wanted German translations **for all texts/for legal texts**.
5. There **was only one vote/were two votes** difference between the pro and the con parties.
6. Muehlenberg voted against the German translation, because he thought that this would **make integration for the German immigrants easier/help Germans and Americans to live together in peace**.

6

## 2 Vocabulary: finding your way through Philadelphia

Fill in the missing words.

**A:** "Hello, can you tell me the way to the African American Museum, please? I have no idea where I am – I have no (1)______________________ of the streets here."

**B:** "Oh yes. It's not very far. First you walk (2)__________________ on, then you should

(3)__________________ the street at the traffic lights over there. Do you see that side street?

(4)__________________ left there! And then you can see it.

**A:** "Thank you very much. I'm so much looking forward to seeing it. It must be really great,

it has a great (5)__________________ . I can't believe that I'll get to see it soon – it's

(6)__________________."

**B:** "It's really one of the best museums here. It shows that the African Americans had a lot of

(7)__________________ and didn't ask for help or support. They had to fight and

(8)__________________ for their rights on their own."

8

## 3 Background knowledge: history

Tick off the correct statement.

1. The War of Independence started as a protest against
   - unfair taxation.
   - violent behavior towards the colonists.
2. George Washington managed to unite
   - all fifteen colonies.
   - all thirteen colonies.
3. In 1776 the leaders of the colonies signed
   - the Declaration of Independence in Philadelphia.
   - the Declaration of War against Britain in Philadelphia.
4. But it took the colonies six more years of war
   - to win over Britain.
   - to find the way across the continent to the Pacific Ocean.
5. By that time, the first slaves
   - had already arrived on the continent.
   - had already settled in Philadelphia.

5

## 4 Grammar: relative clauses

Connect the sentences by using relative clauses. (The second sentence should be turned into a relative clause.) Write down the complete sentences and tick off "N" for a non-defining relative clause and "D" for a defining relative clause.

1. The Liberty Bell is considered a symbol of freedom. The Liberty Bell can be seen in Philadelphia.

   ● N ● D ______________________________________________

   ______________________________________________

2. The guide can tell you many legends about it. A guide waits there for tourists.

   ● N ● D ______________________________________________

   ______________________________________________

3. The tourists say it is amazing. Most tourists visit it.

   ● N ● D ______________________________________________

   ______________________________________________

4. It is located in the Independence National Historical Park. The park is also very popular with tourists.

   ● N ● D ______________________________________________

   ______________________________________________

5. Delaware River is not too far away either. The river was used for the trading ships.

   ● N ● D ______________________________________________

   ______________________________________________

6. Last week a boat sank on Delaware River. The boat had been over-crowded.

   ● N ● D ______________________________________________

   ______________________________________________

___ / 6

## 5 Grammar: the future

Fill in the verbs in the most appropriate form of the future.

When Tony planned a visit to Philadelphia, he wanted to see everything:

1. "I ____________________ (visit) the African American Museum. It must be very interesting!"
2. "If the weather is nice, I ____________________ (take) a little walk through the Independence National Historical Park."
3. "And this afternoon? Oh yes, I ____________________ (meet) my old friend Toby!"
4. "And when should I go back? Here's the timetable – the train back ____________________ (leave) at 5 o'clock."

___ / 4

## 6 Grammar: auxiliaries

In the African American Museum at Philadelphia you can learn a lot about the inhumane living conditions of the slaves. The guide tells you a lot about them, and you talk about them to your friend later, so you use the past.

Guide: "The slaves (1) can't escape. They (2) may marry, but only with the owner's consent. The slaves who work in the household (3) needn't dig up the fields. But the slaves who work on the fields (4) mustn't enter the house. The slaves (5) aren't supposed to talk to the plantation owners. They (6) must stay in their little huts after work. And of course they (7) mustn't learn to read or write."

1. You: "The slaves ______________________________ escape."
2. You: "They ______________________________ marry, but only with the owner's consent."
3. You: "The slaves who worked in the household ______________________________ dig up the fields."
4. You: "But the slaves who worked on the fields ______________________________ enter the house."
5. You: "The slaves ______________________________ talk to the plantation owners."
6. You: "They ______________________________ stay in their little huts after work."
7. You: "And of course they ______________________________ learn to read or write."

7

## 7 Text production: a blog entry

You have just come home from school, where you talked about the Civil Rights Movement and Rosa Parks, who refused to leave her seat in the front of a bus in Alabama, thus starting the fight for equal rights of the African-Americans. Write a blog entry about your impressions of this movement and your school day (about 150 words)! Use your exercise book.

30

80 Gesamtpunkte 80 – 65 Punkte: ☺ 64 – 41 Punkte: 😐 40 – 0 Punkte: ☹

Zeit: 45 min Beginn ______ Ende ______

# The world of work – Test 2

## 1 Listening comprehension: funny jobs

Complete the texts.

1. The diver on golf courses is needed to retrieve the ____________________ of golf balls which end up in the pools every day. This is necessary, because the balls are too expensive to be ____________________ . You must be able ____________________ if you want to get this job. You can earn up to 60 dollars ____________________ .
2. A warm-upper works for a ____________________ . His job is to make the audience happy by, for example, ____________________ . You can earn up to ____________________ dollars for two hours of work, but it is only a ____________________ job.
3. The job as a tester for dog food is great for people who like ____________________ . They are employed by companies which ____________________ dog food. But it's only a part-time job, because there aren't ____________________ different kinds of dog food. The job requires ____________________ qualifications.
4. If you work as a zombie, you go to ____________________ every day. Before you start your work, you must put on some ____________________. Also younger people can do this, because you have to be only ____________________ to apply. But you won't earn too much money – it's only about ____________________ dollars for an eight-hour day.
5. The speaker likes the job of a linestander best, because they needn't do ____________________ . They just have to wait in a line for ____________________ or at museum entrances. You needn't look around for an employer yourself, because there are ____________________ which organize everything. If you want to get this job, you must be old enough, and you must be ____________________ .

____ / 20

## 2 Vocabulary: the world of work

Fill in the missing words. The German words are given in the box, but not in the correct order.

**Angestellte • Belegschaft • Büro • ein eigenes Geschäft führen • erhalten • Fabrik • Gehalt • Schönheitschirurg**

When teenagers think about their future, they all want to earn huge (1)____________________. Some of them want to (2)____________________________ with a lot of (3)_________________. Only few are planning to apply at a (4)____________________ with huge assembly lines. Most prefer to work in an (5)__________. Sometimes, however, they are happy to (6)____________________ a job offer anyway. So they get members of the (7)____________________ of bigger companies. Not everybody will be able to become a (8)____________________.

8

## 3 Background knowledge: history

Fill in the missing words.

When the Declaration of Independence was signed, the cheapest workers had already been brought to the continent – the slaves. There were thousands of them in the (1)____________________ states of the United States. They were needed there as a cheap (2)____________________ to work on the sugar cane and cotton (3)____________________. Their living conditions were extremely awful, and the owners treated them as (4)____________________. When a slave could escape, he sometimes found help from the people of the (5)__________ Railroad.

5

## 4 Grammar: relative clauses

Connect the sentences by using relative clauses. (The second sentence should be turned into a relative clause.) Write down the complete sentences and tick off "N" for a non-defining relative clause and "D" for a defining relative clause.
The supermarket had a lot of trouble with the newspaper carriers last Saturday:

1. John was ill last week. He had started the job only two months ago.

   ● N ● D ________________________________________________________

   ______________________________________________________________

2. The boy didn't find any letterboxes. The boy had moved to Philly two years before.

● N ● D ____________________________________________

____________________________________________

3. The girl couldn't come because her sister was ill. The girl always wears her skates for her round.

● N ● D ____________________________________________

____________________________________________

4. Jenny didn't come either. She's at John's school.

● N ● D ____________________________________________

____________________________________________

5. On Saturday the school did a day trip to the park. Most carriers attend this school.

● N ● D ____________________________________________

____________________________________________

6. The owner of the supermarket nearly went crazy. He is usually very patient.

● N ● D ____________________________________________

____________________________________________

6

## 5 Grammar: the future

Fill in the verbs in the most appropriate form of the future.

John is thinking about applying for a job:

1. "I ________________ (spend) my holidays in Europe."
2. "So I ________________ (need) a lot of money."
3. "I ________________ (buy) a newspaper right now. Maybe there are some job offers in it!"
4. "I can ask Dad, too, when he comes home. His work shift ________________ (finish) at six o'clock."

4

## 6 Grammar: auxiliaries

When Tony started working at the factory, his boss told him what to do. Later he told his girlfriend about the rules.
Fill in the auxiliaries in the past!

Boss: "You (1) are supposed to be here on time. You (2) needn't bring your own shirts. You (3) can wear the company's shirts. But you (4) mustn't wear anything dirty! During lunchtime you (5) may go outside. But you (6) mustn't leave the grounds. If you want to, you (7) can stay longer every day. But you must lock the door when you leave!"

Tony:

1. "We ______________________ here on time."
2. "We ______________________ bring our own shirts."
3. "We ______________________ wear the company's shirts."
4. "But we ______________________ wear anything dirty!"
5. "During lunchtime we ______________________ go outside."
6. "But we ______________________ leave the grounds."
7. "We ______________________ stay longer every day.."

7

## 7 Text production: a job application

You are looking for a summer job. Now you have found the following ad:

Farm helpers needed in August!
We are looking for young people (16 or older)
who can help us in August on our farm!

The job duties include cleaning out the stables
and feeding the animals, but also driving a tractor.
You are supposed to be able to work every day from 9 a.m. to 4 p.m.,
also in bad weather.

Please apply to the Burtons!

This sounds like a great idea, so write the job application.
Write into your exercise book.

30

80 Gesamtpunkte 80 – 64 Punkte: ☺ 63 – 41 Punkte: 😐 40 – 0 Punkte: ☹

# Lösungen

## Theme 1: American high schools

### Seite 12

#### 1 School rules

1. electronic – 2. devices – 3. limited – 4. out of sight – 5. prohibited – 6. trash – 7. disposed of – 8. ID – 9. appropriate – 10. clothing – 11. halls – 12. common – 13. grounds – 14. swear – 15. insult – 16. offensive – 17. manners

#### 2 German-English

ertragen – suffer; Werbung, Reklame – advertising; ansonsten – otherwise; Nachteil – disadvantage; sich (an etwas) bedienen – help oneself; zugeben, anerkennen – acknowledge; kritisieren – criticize; übertreiben – exaggerate; käuflich erwerben – purchase; Verantwortung – responsibility

#### 3 Expressing your opinion

Example

1. As far as I'm concerned I don't use my cell phone at school anyway.
2. Personally, I think that apple pie is the best thing I've ever had!
3. I have to admit that there is really a lot of trash in the streets downtown.
4. I'd say that there are also great schools in the USA!

#### 4 Karl's first week

1. did you like – 2. has been – 3. met – 4. have invited – 5. usually don't go – 6. am going to go – 7. will have – 8. went – 9. had bought – 10. was dancing – 11. spilled – 12. had to throw – 13. Are you going to come – 14. haven't been invited – 15. will call – 16. is taking part

#### 5 Present perfect and simple past

The correct forms are:

1. has brought – 2. bought/ate – 3. has put – 4. wanted/hasn't washed – 5. has been invited – 6. has even bought/was completely ruined

#### 6 Present perfect progressive

1. He has been playing football for three years.
2. He has been working for the school magazine since 2013.
3. She has been dancing in the cheerleader group since 2012.
4. She has (only) been acting for six months.

#### 7 be supposed to/be expected to

1. are expected to/are supposed to – 2. mustn't – 3. are expected to/are supposed to – 4. needn't – 5. must

#### 8 Connectives

1. because: The Powder Puff football game was a great success for Lake Park High School, because their team won 79–35.
2. although: Patton High School was defeated, although they had scored 12 points in the first minutes.
3. due to: Lake Park's Lancers had great support due to their fantastic fans.
4. so: Debby Mayers scored 24 points, so she was the best player.
5. thanks to: The Susan G. Komen Breast Cancer Foundation is supported by Lake Park High School thanks to the money from the match.

#### 9 Chicago – the Windy City

1. true – 2. false – 3. true – 4. false – 5. true – 6. false – 7. true – 8. false – 9. true – 10. false – 11. true – 12. false

#### 10 Cheerleaders

1. five – 2. invites – 3. opinion – 4. Hollywood movies 5. stupid – 6. unfair/mean – 7. thin

#### 11 Rules

Example

From: karl@german.de – To: harrington@lakepark.us
Subject: school rules in Germany
Dear Mrs Harrington,
When we met last week, you asked me about the rules at my school in Germany. You won't be surprised that there are strict rules, too. The most important ones are even the same!
Like here, all students are supposed to come to school on time, which means 8 o'clock. In Germany, school usually starts at 8 o'clock, but there are not so many lessons in the afternoon. Moreover, the use of electronic devices is forbidden, too. We are expected to turn our smartphones off and put them out of sight, too. And of course there are rules concerning the appropriate behavior at school like here. We mustn't, for example, throw trash around, but dispose of it in a proper way.
But there are also differences. Maybe you know that in Germany there are usually no school uniforms, although the students often have the opportunity to wear school t-shirts. This would be very strange for you!
You see, not all rules will be new for me at Lake Park High School. Thank you again for your help!
Best regards,
Karl

#### 12 Personal statement

Example

Dear Mr McSweeny,
I am new at Lake Park High School, and I would like to join your soccer team.
I have been playing soccer for ten years in Germany, in the club in my home town and at school, so I usually play soccer three times a week. Due to this, I would really miss the training sessions, and your soccer team would therefore be a great opportunity for me to have regular training.

In Germany soccer is very popular. I think that to be good at soccer you must not only be a great athlete, but also a good team player, and thanks to this the matches are always very exciting.
You see, I don't only play myself, also I often go to the matches of the big clubs. Personally I am a great fan of FC Bayern München. Therefore I know the rules and situations quite well, and maybe I could tell the other team members more about this sport, too.
I'm looking forward to hearing from you.
Best regards,
Karl

### 13 Article for the school magazine

Example
**YEE HAW for the coolest cowboys in town!**
When I arrived at Lake Park High School on Tuesday during Homecoming Week, I couldn't believe my eyes: I found myself in the middle of Texas! The halls and grounds were filled with "YEE HAW" shouts and cowboys were running around everywhere.
Not only the students, but also the teachers had put on their best western wear. They really enjoyed wearing their cowboy hats – even during lessons. And the students did so, too. "It's great fun to see all the teachers in their cowboy hats", one student said.
This homecoming event was a good idea to bring together students and teachers once again. Everybody took part in the fun and laughed together, and it was a great opportunity to see the others from a different point of view.
Although "Texas Tuesday" is such a phenomenal day, some students overdid the fun a little. What fun is it, when students don't stop shouting in the lessons and go wild during the breaks? That is a real pity, because there are people who don't like the day – there are "more important things to do at school", as Mrs Harrington said.
But if you look at all the fun and the great atmosphere, it's no question that the day was huge success – and coach McSweeny has already promised to bring his cowboy hat again next year!

### 14 Email

Example:
From: karl@german.de – To: harrington@lakepark.us
Subject: school rules in Germany
Dear Mrs Harrington,
When we met last week, you asked me to write you an email about my first days at Lake Park High School.
My first impressions were really good. I have to admit that I was a bit worried because there are so many students and some things are different to my German school. But everybody was so friendly and helpful that I felt at home quite soon.
And the sports program at Lake Park is really great! There are so many opportunities to take part in sports that it's hard for me to decide which team I'm going to join.
Personally I think that the soccer team would be a good idea for me, because I have already been playing soccer in Germany for five years. But I would also love to try out bowling, football or baseball, because these sports are not very popular in Germany. This would be a great chance for me to learn about these sports.
I have already learned a lot about American schools and of course about Chicago. My host sister Laura has taken me to different places, and I think I like the famous skyline best. It's such a great view!
I'm really happy to be here. Thank you again for your support on my first days.
Best regards,
Karl

## Lösungen zur Klassenarbeit At Lake Park High School – Test 1

### Seite 23

Soweit nicht anders angegeben, gib dir für jede richtig gelöste Teilaufgabe einen Punkt. Bei Lückentexten gibt es für jede richtig gefüllte Lücke einen Punkt. Bei Rechtschreibfehlern ziehe dir für jeden Fehler einen halben Punkt ab.
Beachte auch die weiteren Bewertungshinweise.

### 1 Listening comprehension: school spirit

I.
1. In the USA students go to school **to live**.
2. At American high schools, sport is something **really important**.
3. In the USA, young people do sports mostly **at high school**.
4. In the USA, school lessons usually start at **8 o'clock**.
5. All teams have training sessions for two or three hours **a day**.
6. golf, cheerleading or tennis (baseball, basketball, track and field, softball, soccer, volleyball, swimming)
7. try-outs, training sessions on three or four days
8. in one season, in spring, fall or winter

II. respected – hard – support – halls – buildings or cars

III. Correct sentences: The parents are very interested in their children's teams. The parents drive very long ways to watch the matches. The students are often less excited than their parents. The schools can't pay their teams much money. The parents must pay a lot of money for the outfits, especially for cheerleaders.
Give yourself one credit for each correct sentence! Take off one credit if you have ticked off a wrong sentence!

### 2 Vocabulary: Mrs Harrington

staff – located – attend – sophomore – sufficiently – nurse – join – grade

### 3 Grammar: simple past/present perfect
gave – have met – has invited – Have you seen – talked – have never seen

### 4 Grammar: present perfect progressive
has been standing – Have you already packed – have been learning – have been working – have you told – have been playing

### 5 Grammar: mixed tenses
1. Did you see – 2. was standing – 3. had passed – 4. has anybody seen – 5. have been looking – 6. am packing – 7. is going to go – 8. has invited – 9. win – 10. will give

### 6 Text production: newspaper article (mediation)
Korrigiere deinen Text oder lasse ihn von jemandem korrigieren und verteile bis zu 10 Punkte (credits = cr.) für jeden Bereich anhand der folgenden Kriterien:
Form:
9–10 cr.: Überschrift ist kurz und treffend, Text ist in Abschnitte eingeteilt, im ersten Abschnitt werden die wichtigen Fragen (Wer? Was? Wann? Wo? Warum?) beantwortet, durchgehender roter Faden erkennbar, persönliche Haltung erkennbar, Ton ist für Leser passend gewählt.
7–8 cr.: Überschrift ist sehr lang, Abschnitte fehlen manchmal, der Einstieg ist langweilig, einzelne Fragen bleiben unbeantwortet, ab und zu fehlen Übergänge.
5–6 cr.: Überschrift besteht aus ganzem Satz und passt nicht genau zum Thema, einige Fragen werden nicht beantwortet, Abschnitte fehlen, Zusammenhänge sind nicht immer verständlich.
3–4 cr.: Keine oder unpassende Überschrift, im ersten Abschnitt werden nur einzelne Fragen beantwortet, Zusammenhänge fehlen oft, persönliche Haltung nur selten erkennbar.
1–2 cr.: Keine oder unpassende Überschrift, keine Absätze, im ersten Abschnitt werden wichtige Fragen nicht beantwortet, kein roter Faden erkennbar, keine persönliche Haltung erkennbar, Ton trifft Anlass nicht.
Inhalt:
9–10 cr.: Informationen sind gezielt für einen allgemeinen Artikel über eine solche Tradition ausgewählt, Unnötiges ist weggelassen (z. B. Namen), alle Quellen sind einbezogen, spannende und lebendige Einzelheiten sind ergänzt, Gedankengang ist schlüssig und nachvollziehbar.
7–8 cr.: Einzelne Informationen fehlen, einzelne unnötige Details sind übernommen, Gedankengang ist an einzelnen Stellen unklar.
5–6 cr.: Im Großen und Ganzen sind die wichtigen Informationen vorhanden, der Gedankengang ist bis auf einige Stellen klar, Informationen sind manchmal oberflächlich dargestellt, einzelne Wiederholungen treten auf.
3–4 cr.: Informationen fehlen oder sind an einzelnen Stellen falsch, einzelne Quellen sind nicht bearbeitet, nur pauschale Behauptungen ohne interessante Ausschmückungen sind vorhanden, Informationen werden aneinandergereiht.
1–2 cr.: Informationen sind falsch übernommen, zu viele Details sind übernommen, Informationen sind nur pauschal und oberflächlich wiedergegeben, Wiederholungen treten auf, Gedankengang ist wirr.
Sprache:
9–10 cr.: Sprachlich fehlerfrei, ganz selten Rechtschreibfehler, abwechslungsreiche Formulierungen, keine Wortwiederholungen, Sätze sind mit Nebensätzen gebildet und hängen zusammen.
7–8 cr.: Einzelne Fehler in Wortschatz oder Grammatik (z. B. *tenses*), manchmal werden Wörter wiederholt, einzelne Sätze sind nicht verknüpft.
5–6 cr.: Einfache Sätze ohne Nebensätze, häufige Fehler in Wortschatz und Grammatik (v. a. *tenses*, Satzbau), nur ganz selten sind Sätze verknüpft.
3–4 cr.: An einzelnen Stellen ist der Text unverständlich, weil falsche oder deutsche Wörter verwendet werden oder die Grammatik völlig falsch verwendet ist.
1–2 cr.: Text ist über weite Strecken unverständlich, falsche oder deutsche Wörter werden verwendet, Grammatik wird (fast) durchgehend falsch verwendet.
Example
Who's the boss?
Many different school teams, hot Friday night matches, loud cheering for your team – this is what I first saw at my new American school. My German school has only got one big sports event: the soccer match between teachers and students.
It takes place at the end of every school year and everybody is invited.
Usually the teachers have mixed teams with men and women together – after all, there are not so many teachers at German schools. And maybe the teachers are too slow and old for the healthy and strong students. Fact is that year after year the teachers are defeated. Thanks to the audience there is always a lot of fun. All the students are invited and because the matches take place in the morning, there are no lessons. (Maybe this is also the reason why everybody loves these matches!)
Sometimes even the school band plays during half time, and after the match the teams meet and have a kind of party. This shows that the match is important to all players, but in the end it's all about fun.

## Lösungen zur Klassenarbeit People and Places in Chicago – Test 2

### Seite 27

Soweit nicht anders angegeben, gib dir für jede richtig gelöste Teilaufgabe einen Punkt. Bei Lückentexten gibt es für jede richtig gefüllte Lücke einen Punkt. Bei Rechtschreibfehlern ziehe dir für jeden Fehler einen halben Punkt ab.
Beachte auch die weiteren Bewertungshinweise.

### 1 Reading comprehension: Al Capone
I.
1. Everybody knows who Al Capone was.
2. Al Capone committed many crimes in Chicago.
3. His parents had nine children.
4. He left school after eight years.
5. Growing up in New York was very hard at that time.
6. Al Capone was born in 1899.
7. After a bad street fight he had a huge scar in his face.

II. moved, went away – illegally – stop – street, place – a gang – hide – the police, politicians – protected;

III.

1. gave money to poor people, was seen as a kind of modern Robin Hood
2. owned a furniture shop
3. invest illegal money (in a legal shop)
4. hadn't paid his taxes
5. there are many books and films about him

## 2 Vocabulary: the Black Socks scandal

shows off – played against – defeat – in a row – responsibility – swore – disadvantages – purchase

## 3 Grammar: simple past/present perfect

1. have you already cleaned – 2. walked – 3. have seen – 4. gave – 5. took

## 4 Grammar: present perfect progressive

1. has just finished – 2. has been working – 3. has found – 4. has been doing – 5. hasn't cleaned – 6. has been cleaning

## 5 Grammar: mixed tenses

1. have been invited – 2. didn't play – 3. started – 4. was raining – 5. left – 6. had been great – 7. has found – 8. is reading – 9. is going to buy – 10. will have – 11. is going to come

## 6 Text production: email

Korrigiere deinen Text oder lasse ihn von jemandem korrigieren und verteile bis zu 10 Punkte (credits = cr.) für jeden Bereich anhand der folgenden Kriterien:

Form:

9–10 cr.: Begrüßung, Schlussformel und „Unterschrift" sind vorhanden, im ersten Satz wird der Anlass genannt, im letzten Satz wird ein angemessener Ausblick gegeben; Text ist weitgehend in sinnvolle Abschnitte gegliedert, durchgehend ist ein roter Faden erkennbar, durchgehend wird der Adressat angesprochen, Ton ist passend.

7–8 cr.: Ein Teil einer Mail fehlt, im ersten Satz fehlt ein passender Einstieg, die Mail hört abrupt auf, ansonsten ist der Text in Abschnitte gegliedert, ein roter Faden ist erkennbar, der Adressat wird angesprochen.

5–6 cr.: Zwei Teile einer Mail fehlen, der Text beginnt zusammenhanglos mit einer Information, der Adressat wird kaum angesprochen, Absätze fehlen, meistens sind die Zusammenhänge unklar.

3–4 cr.: Mehrere Teile einer Mail fehlen, es werden keine Absätze gebildet, der Adressat wird kaum angesprochen, unterschiedliche Informationen stehen zusammenhanglos nebeneinander.

1–2 cr.: Form entspricht nicht einem üblichen Brief, keine Absätze vorhanden, keine direkte Anrede an den Adressaten erkennbar.

Inhalt:

9–10 cr.: Alle vorgegebenen Themen sind angesprochen und mit eigenen Ideen ausgebaut, die Informationen sind korrekt und schlüssig, der Adressat wird persönlich angesprochen, die eigene Haltung des Schreibers wird deutlich.

7–8 cr.: Eines der vorgegebenen Themen ist nur genannt, ohne dass darauf näher eingegangen wird, die Aussagen sind weitgehend persönlich und originell, der Adressat wird meistens angesprochen.

5–6 cr.: Im Großen und Ganzen sind die wichtigen Informationen vorhanden, der Gedankengang ist bis auf einige Stellen klar, die Aussagen sind streckenweise oberflächlich und sehr pauschal, einzelne Wiederholungen treten auf.

3–4 cr.: Informationen fehlen oder sind an einzelnen Stellen falsch, nur pauschale Behauptungen ohne interessante Ausschmückungen sind vorhanden, Informationen werden aneinandergereiht, kein Adressatenbezug erkennbar.

1–2 cr.: Informationen sind falsch oder fehlen ganz, Aussagen sind nur pauschal und oberflächlich, Wiederholungen treten auf, Gedankengang ist wirr, Adressatenbezug fehlt ganz.

Sprache:

9–10 cr.: Sprachlich fehlerfrei, ganz selten Rechtschreibfehler, abwechslungsreiche Formulierungen, keine Wortwiederholungen, Sätze sind mit Nebensätzen gebildet und hängen zusammen.

7–8 cr.: Einzelne Fehler in Wortschatz oder Grammatik (z.B. *tenses*), manchmal werden Wörter wiederholt, einzelne Sätze sind nicht verknüpft.

5–6 cr.: Einfache Sätze ohne Nebensätze, häufige Fehler in Wortschatz und Grammatik (v. a. *tenses*, Satzbau), nur ganz selten sind Sätze verknüpft.

3–4 cr.: An einzelnen Stellen ist der Text unverständlich, weil falsche oder deutsche Wörter verwendet werden oder die Grammatik völlig falsch verwendet ist.

1–2 cr.: Text ist über weite Strecken unverständlich, falsche oder deutsche Wörter werden verwendet, Grammatik wird (fast) durchgehend falsch verwendet.

Example

from: nick@pulaski.us – to: taylor@smith.us

subject: my new host brother Karl

Hi Taylor,

You've asked me to write about my new host brother Karl. He's really a nice guy, you know, although he's a bit older than me.

But the first days with him were great. I took him to downtown Chicago – you know I like showing off with my city! And guess what? He didn't like Navy Pier that much! He said that there were better parks in Germany! But I bet he has never seen such a skyline from a ferris wheel in Germany before!

And can you imagine that in Germany they only have a few sports teams at school? And they don't play baseball at all. You know I couldn't do without baseball for a single year. And no Friday night games! All they play is soccer, soccer and soccer. Isn't that boring? I have to admit it sounds like an interesting game, but it's so complicated. I wonder if Karl will still like soccer after he has seen the Bears!

So you see everything is fine here. And maybe I will come to New York and visit you with Karl in summer!

Bye,

Nick

# Theme 2: Wyoming

## Seite 32

### 1 Wordsearch

| | | | | | | | | | | | | | | |
|---|---|---|---|---|---|---|---|---|---|---|---|---|---|---|
| A | C | E | N | T | S | E | B | H | I | N | S | T | E | G |
| H | N | E | A | B | U | S | E | A | S | T | M | E | N | S |
| E | S | T | I | B | I | L | N | S | V | A | G | S | O | M |
| N | O | V | E | S | C | A | P | E | S | T | L | I | C | K |
| T | N | A | R | B | I | V | S | A | T | P | A | M | E | S |
| C | I | N | O | R | D | E | R | T | O | O | C | M | S | T |
| A | B | C | S | H | E | M | S | T | R | I | K | I | N | G |
| B | N | I | S | T | C | H | V | A | S | N | T | G | E | S |
| N | O | E | V | I | L | S | T | C | A | T | O | R | I | V |
| C | H | N | R | E | S | A | B | K | N | C | K | A | M | T |
| T | O | T | I | S | H | C | M | E | N | S | T | N | E | I |
| V | I | S | B | O | U | M | V | O | S | A | N | T | R | S |

attack – in order to – vibrant – ancient – lack – point – evil – immigrant – striking – suicide – escape – abuse - slave

### 2 Describing pictures: Thanksgiving

1. in the middle – 2. On the left-hand side – 3. on the right-hand side – 4. In the foreground – 5. In the background – 6. in the top left-hand corner – 7. At the top – 8. in the bottom righ-hand corner

### 3 The passive voice: different tenses

1. is told – 2. are given – 3. was taken – 4. had been hurt – 5. will be given

### 4 The passive voice: infinitives with or without *to*

You had to circle:
1. to be given – 2. be won – 3. to be looked down on – 4. be left – 5. to be looked after

### 5 Past perfect simple/progressive

1. had packed – 2. had been looking – 3. had been talking – 4. had forgotten – 5. had thanked/had been supporting

### 6 Sacajawea

Correct sentences: Some women were married to cowboys. Some women could even shoot brilliantly. She could speak with the Indians and stop them when they planned an attack. During the expedition she met her own family. Without her the expedition would not have been successful. The Native Americans of the Wind River reservation in Wyoming are very proud of her.

### 7 College rodeo

1. one year – 2. State – 3. easy – 4. trouble/problems – 5. many years – 6. two students/one boy and one girl – 7. High School Rodeo – 8. religious – 9. grew up – 10. happy/glad

### 8 Analyzing pictures

Example
The picture shows a run-down place in a Native Indian reservation today.
In the foreground you can see a little house which looks quite poor. The other buildings on the picture look run-down too. These houses are located in the middle of land, which looks very dry. There are no trees or fields. In the background you can see a huge rock. The inhabitants of one of the houses are sitting on the front porch next so some garbage. They seem to be idle.
The picture shows the poor living conditions of the Native Americans who still live in reservations today. There are not many jobs, so people don't have much money and only little hope for the future.
I think the picture shows a true, but exaggerated image of life in the reservations, because there have been programs to support the Native Americans, although there are still many problems.

### 9 Debate

Example
You say that a visit to a rodeo show offers the opportunity to many young people to learn about animals. I have to admit that many teenagers today don't know much about nature. But I don't think these young people live in places like Douglas, where there are horses or other animals everywhere. So I'm convinced that for most students at High School in Douglas it's just not necessary to spend a whole day just watching some guys riding horses.
Moreover, this visit would be very expensive. The students would have to pay for the transport and for the food, and not everything can be paid for by the school. It might not be much money, but people have to pay for it anyway, whether they want to or not. So I think that a complete day off for everybody would be too expensive for an activity which doesn't teach the students much.

### 10 Newspaper article

Example
**The traditional turkey – not for Germans!**
If you are German and your are in the USA for the first time over Thanksgiving weekend, you will be surprised about this holiday.
It's true – there are holidays, too, where the family members meet and have dinner together with traditional food. Usually it's Christmas that is celebrated in this way. But a holiday with parades like Macy's Parade in New York? And visits to football matches?
This is something very special in the USA. And it's no surprise, because the holiday comes from a time in American history which is completely different to the European history. So why should Germans celebrate Thanksgiving like that?

It's nevertheless unusual. And it's nevertheless a great experience for everybody who has never spent the Thanksgiving weekend in the USA before!

# Lösungen zur Klassenarbeit Pocahontas – Test 1

## Seite 39

Soweit nicht anders angegeben, gib dir für jede richtig gelöste Teilaufgabe einen Punkt. Bei Lückentexten gibt es für jede richtig gefüllte Lücke einen Punkt. Bei Rechtschreibfehlern ziehe dir für jeden Fehler einen halben Punkt ab.
Beachte auch die weiteren Bewertungshinweise.

### 1 Reading comprehension: Pocahontas

I. 1. r – 2. w – 3. w – 4. r – 5. w – 6. w
II. 1. 18 – 2. Rebecca – 3. Europeans/people in Jamestown/Englishmen – 4. political – 5. nice/friendly – 6. beautiful – 7. England/London/Europe – 8. proud
III. 1. 1580 – 2. 1607 – 3. Pocahontas married John Rolfe. – 4. 1615 – 5. Pocahontas died. – 6. Disney released the film "Pocahontas".

### 2 Vocabulary: Native Americans

1. settlers – 2. founded – 3. tribes – 4. both ... and – 5. meat – 6. spread – 7. beliefs – 8. danger – 9. poverty – 10. unemployment

### 3 Describing pictures: Pocahontas meets Captain Smith

1. In the middle of the picture/In the foreground – 2. in the top right-hand corner – 3. On the left-hand side – 4. In the bottom left-hand corner – 5. on the right-hand side

### 4 Grammar: passive – different tenses

1. was loved – 2. have been seen – 3. have been told – 4. was visited – 5. had been told

### 5 Grammar: passive – infinitives with or without *to*

to be looked – to be left – are given – to be given – be taught

### 6 Grammar: past perfect simple/progressive

1. had been sailing – 2. had shouted – 3. had never seen – 4. had been watching – 5. had been living

### 7 Text production: debate

Korrigiere deinen Text oder lasse ihn von jemandem korrigieren und verteile bis zu 10 Punkte (credits = cr.) für jeden Bereich anhand der folgenden Kriterien:
Form:
9–10 cr.: Der Text ist in Abschnitte eingeteilt; im ersten Abschnitt wird die vorige Äußerung aufgegriffen und kommentiert; roter Faden erkennbar, der Inhalt ist logisch aufgebaut.
7–8 cr.: Manchmal sind keine Abschnitte gemacht, der Einstieg wiederholt nur die vorige Äußerung, der Gedankengang ist manchmal wirr.
5–6 cr.: Abschnitte sind meistens in Ordnung, Einstieg wiederholt nur die vorige Äußerung, nicht alle Teile sind sinnvoll verknüpft, ab und zu fehlen Überleitungen oder Erklärungen, einzelne Informationen werden wiederholt
3–4 cr.: Im ersten Abschnitt wird nur pauschal auf die vorige Äußerung eingegangen, die Inhalte sind unverknüpft nebeneinander gestellt, Gründe werden nur aufgezählt, die eigene Meinung wird nicht deutlich gesagt.
1–2 cr.: Im ersten Abschnitt wird die vorige Äußerung gar nicht berücksichtigt, Informationen werden nur aufgezählt, kein roter Faden ist erkennbar, die eigene Meinung bleibt unklar.
Inhalt:
9–10 cr.: Im ersten Abschnitt wird die vorige Äußerung geschickt paraphrasiert und mit eigenem Inhalt kommentiert, die eigene Meinung wird mit zwei sinnvollen Gründen erläutert, die Gründe sind überzeugend mit Beispielen ausgestaltet.
7–8 cr.: Im ersten Abschnitt wird auf die vorige Äußerung eingegangen, die eigene Meinung wird mit zwei sinnvollen Gründen erläutert, die Gründe sind nicht immer überzeugend mit Beispielen ausgestaltet.
5–6 cr.: Im ersten Abschnitt wird die vorige Äußerung nur wiederholt, die eigene Meinung wird nur pauschal gesagt, die Gründe sind zum Teil schwach ausgesucht und nicht sehr überzeugend mit Beispielen ausgestaltet.
3–4 cr.: Im ersten Abschnitt wird nur pauschal auf die vorige Äußerung eingegangen, die eigene Meinung wird kaum deutlich, mindestens einer der Gründe ist sehr schwach, die Beispiele sind sehr einfach oder zeigen Einzelfälle.
1–2 cr.: Kein Bezug zur vorigen Äußerung, eigene Meinung wird nicht deutlich, mindestens ein Grund fehlt ganz, sehr einfache oder gar keine Beispiele.
Sprache:
9–10 cr.: Sprachlich fehlerfrei, ganz selten Rechtschreibfehler, abwechslungsreiche Formulierungen, keine Wortwiederholungen, Sätze sind mit Nebensätzen gebildet und hängen zusammen.
7–8 cr.: Einzelne Fehler in Wortschatz oder Grammatik (z. B. *tenses*), manchmal werden Wörter wiederholt, einzelne Sätze sind nicht verknüpft.
5–6 cr.: Einfache Sätze ohne Nebensätze, häufige Fehler in Wortschatz und Grammatik (v. a. *tenses*, Satzbau), nur ganz selten sind Sätze verknüpft.
3–4 cr.: An einzelnen Stellen ist der Text unverständlich, weil falsche oder deutsche Wörter verwendet werden oder die Grammatik völlig falsch verwendet ist.
1–2 cr.: Text ist über weite Strecken unverständlich, falsche oder deutsche Wörter werden verwendet, Grammatik wird (fast) durchgehend falsch verwendet.

Example
Marcy, you say that the Native Americans shouldn't be given the money because it is not enough money to help them. Do you really think that this will convince the people in the reservation? Is a little money not better than no money?
Just imagine the projects they could do with it! They could build a little playground for the children. And a small basketball court could be built for the teenagers so that they needn't stay at home anymore.
I'm really convinced that even if it is not much money it will help the Native Americans much more than the students at High School. Do they really need a new library? Don't they use the internet? Just look at us! We are "talking" online, we are getting information online, and we meet online. Nobody wants to read books

anymore! So I am really convinced that the money should be given to the reservation.

## Lösungen zur Klassenarbeit Wild Wild West – Test 2

### Seite 44

Soweit nicht anders angegeben, gib dir für jede richtig gelöste Teilaufgabe einen Punkt. Bei Lückentexten gibt es für jede richtig gefüllte Lücke einen Punkt. Bei Rechtschreibfehlern ziehe dir für jeden Fehler einen halben Punkt ab.
Beachte auch die weiteren Bewertungshinweise.

#### 1 Listening comprehension: Buffalo Bill

I. 1. William Frederick Cody – 2. wrote stories about him – 3. rode the horses – 4. the wars/battles against the Indians – 5. lost his hat (and part of the skin of his head) – 6. worked for/built the railroad to the West – 7. killed 4280 buffalo in 18 months/many buffalo –

II.

9. In 1872 Buffalo Bill was invited to play himself in "Scouts of the Prairie".
10. Buffalo Bill's Wild West Show became very popular, because many famous cowboys or even Native Americans took part.
11. Sitting Bull's father took him out to hunt buffalo when he was 10 years old.
12. In the wars against the whites Sitting Bull was the head of a huge army of Native Americans.
13. In the battle of the Little Big Horn in 1876 the Native Americans were very successful.
14. When he went to Germany with his show in 1891, Buffalo Bill caused great interest in the Wild West.
15. Although his show had been very successful in Europe, he lost nearly all his money after about 30 years.
16. The small town Cody in Wyoming was founded by Buffalo Bill himself.

III. A: Cody was born. – B: 1860 – C: end of Civil War – D: 1865 – E: 1869

#### 2 Vocabulary: going west

1. trails – 2. fertile – 3. community – 4. crimes – 5. drunk – 6. holidays – 7. dedication – 8. landmarks – 9. association – 10. on average

#### 3 Describing pictures: after Little Big Horn

1. In the background – 2. On the right-hand side – 3. in the bottom right-hand corner – 4. In the middle/In the foreground – 5. On the left-hand side

#### 4 Grammar: passive – different tenses

1. was greeted – 2. were interested – 3. had been brought – 4. have been shown – 5. have already been asked

#### 5 Grammar: passive – infinitives with or without *to*

1. to be seen – 2. to be given – 3. to be named – 4. be put – 5. be told

#### 6 Grammar: past perfect simple/progressive

1. had been traveling – 2. had just visited – 3. had been talking – 4. had found – 5. had been digging

#### 7 Text production: newspaper article (mediation)

Korrigiere deinen Text oder lasse ihn von jemandem korrigieren und verteile bis zu 10 Punkte (credits = cr.) für jeden Bereich anhand der folgenden Kriterien:
Form:
9–10 cr.: Überschrift ist kurz und treffend, Text ist in Abschnitte eingeteilt, im ersten Abschnitt werden die wichtigen Fragen (Wer? Was? Wann? Wo? Warum?) beantwortet, durchgehender roter Faden erkennbar, persönliche Haltung erkennbar, Ton ist für Leser passend gewählt.
7–8 cr.: Überschrift ist sehr lang, Abschnitte fehlen manchmal, der Einstieg ist langweilig, einzelne Fragen bleiben unbeantwortet, ab und zu fehlen Übergänge.
5–6 cr.: Überschrift besteht aus ganzem Satz und passt nicht genau zum Thema, einige Fragen werden nicht beantwortet, Abschnitte fehlen, Zusammenhänge sind nicht immer verständlich.
3–4 cr.: Keine oder unpassende Überschrift, im ersten Abschnitt werden nur einzelne Fragen beantwortet, Zusammenhänge fehlen oft, persönliche Haltung nur selten erkennbar.
1–2 cr.: Keine oder unpassende Überschrift, keine Absätze, im ersten Abschnitt werden wichtige Fragen nicht beantwortet, kein roter Faden erkennbar, keine persönliche Haltung erkennbar, Ton trifft Anlass nicht.
Inhalt:
9–10 cr.: Informationen sind gezielt für einen allgemeinen Artikel über Western City ausgewählt, Unnötiges ist weggelassen (z.B. Namen), alle Quellen sind einbezogen, spannende und lebendige Einzelheiten sind ergänzt, Gedankengang ist schlüssig und nachvollziehbar.
7–8 cr.: Einzelne Informationen fehlen, einzelne unnötige Details sind übernommen, Gedankengang ist an einzelnen Stellen unklar.
5–6 cr.: Im Großen und Ganzen sind die wichtigen Informationen vorhanden, der Gedankengang ist bis auf einige Stellen klar, Informationen sind manchmal oberflächlich dargestellt, einzelne Wiederholungen treten auf.
3–4 cr.: Informationen fehlen oder sind an einzelnen Stellen falsch, einzelne Quellen sind nicht bearbeitet, nur pauschale Behauptungen ohne interessante Ausschmückungen sind vorhanden, Informationen werden aneinandergereiht.
1–2 cr.: Informationen sind falsch übernommen, zu viele Details sind übernommen, Informationen sind nur pauschal und oberflächlich wiedergegeben, Wiederholungen treten auf, Gedankengang ist wirr.
Sprache:
9–10 cr.: Sprachlich fehlerfrei, ganz selten Rechtschreibfehler, abwechslungsreiche Formulierungen, keine Wortwiederholungen, Sätze sind mit Nebensätzen gebildet und hängen zusammen.
7–8 cr.: Einzelne Fehler in Wortschatz oder Grammatik (z.B. *tenses*), manchmal werden Wörter wiederholt, einzelne Sätze sind nicht verknüpft.
5–6 cr.: Einfache Sätze ohne Nebensätze, häufige Fehler in Wortschatz und Grammatik (v.a. *tenses*, Satzbau), nur ganz selten sind Sätze verknüpft.
3–4 cr.: An einzelnen Stellen ist der Text unverständlich, weil falsche oder deutsche Wörter verwendet werden oder die Grammatik völlig falsch verwendet ist.

1–2 cr.: Text ist über weite Strecken unverständlich, falsche oder deutsche Wörter werden verwendet, Grammatik wird (fast) durchgehend falsch verwendet.

Example

**Become a cowboy for one day!**

To live the life of a cowboy, rancher or even Indian is the big dream of almost every little boy or girl. At the Western City in Neuberg you can do that, at least for one day!

You can take part in many different western activities, while people from the Wild West watch and count your credits. You can, for example, throw a lasso, set up traps or throw knives. If you want to experience the life of an Indian you can bow-hunt or even watch one of the famous Indian dances. Don't forget to let the sheriff, the cowboy, the Indian or the trapper mark your results on your ticket which you get at the entrance!

When you are tired after all these games you can visit the museum or even watch a movie at the cinema.

Even if you come from America and think you know everything about the Wild Wild West – this place is worth a visit! You can learn so much about your country's history. Furthermore you can enjoy a great day filled with spectacular shows and funny games! A visit at the Western City is really a great way to spend your holidays or your weekend.

# Theme 3: New York

## Seite 49

### 1 Feelings

1. ~~ecstatic~~, negative – 2. ~~relieved~~, negative – 3. ~~desperate~~, positive – 4. ~~annoyed~~, positive

### 2 American English/British English

Parkplatz – car park (BE)
French fries (AE) – chips (BE)
Laden/Geschäft – store (AE)
Keks – biscuit (BE)

### 3 The weather

1. sunny – 2. cloudy – 3. snowfall

### 4 Gerund constructions

The correct forms are:
1. about going – 2. to seeing – 3. on visiting – 4. of going – 5. for finding

### 5 Gerund or infinitive?

1. to buy – 2. to drink – 3. using – 4. imitating – 5. teaching

### 6 Sentence adverbs

You had to circle:
1. First of all – 2. Afterwards – 3. Just when – 4. immediately

### 7 Revision: questions

1. Where can we get something to drink? – 2. Do you like New York? – 3. Can you stay here for two more weeks? – 4. won't you? – 5. can't you? – 6. doesn't it? – 7. aren't they – 8. haven't you – 9. don't we – 10. isn't it

### 8 Revision: comparison of adjectives

1. best – 2. more gigantic – 3. friendlier

### 9 Central Park

1. wrong – 2. wrong – 3. right – 4. wrong – 5. right – 6. wrong – 7. wrong – 8. right

### 10 Christmas shopping

1. ... he thinks she is difficult. – 2. ... his sister Betty has got so many already. – 3. ... they think book stores are boring. – 4. ... they are too expensive. – 5. ... he wants to see the decorations. – 6. ... he wants to see the tree. – 7. ... it's very cold.

### 11 Online chat

Example:

Maureen: Hey, how's your shopping going? Have you found anything for me already? ☺

Catriona: Well, not really. We wanted to go to Macy's alright, but there was so much to see ... Window shopping in New York is really unbelievable! Everything glitters and shines, and there are even moving decorations. It is very exhausting, isn't it?

Maureen: Poor you! Is Macy's really as big as everybody says?

Catriona: Well, to me it seemed as big as all the shops in Ireland put together! It's incredible! We spent about five hours there and I couldn't decide on one single present for you. And after that we went to one of the christmas markets, too.

Maureen: You don't say! Are there really christmas markets in New York? They can't be as nice as our good old market here! We missed you a lot, when we had our usual cup of tea there.

Catriona: I can't believe it. You really went there without me? How annoying!

Maureen: Well, next year you'll be here again ...

### 12 Audio guide

Example:

Here we are in an area that seems quite crowded – and everyone looks Asian. Just take a closer look: you'll see mothers and their children playing in the streets, you'll see bright red posters with Chinese signs on them, you'll see strange instruments that you have never seen before. And it's no surprise that most people here look Asian: we're in the middle of Chinatown!

In the 19th century most immigrants came from European countries (and especially Germany), but times have changed. Today most immigrants come from Mexico – and from Asian countries. In the bigger cities of the USA you will find whole communities of Asian people living together in the same part of the city. There are even districts that are called "Chinatown". But there aren't only immigrants from China. Today many immigrants also come from the Philippines, Korea or Vietnam. And they all have brought their own culture with them!

## Lösungen zur Klassenarbeit Ellis Island – Test 1

### Seite 56

Soweit nicht anders angegeben, gib dir für jede richtig gelöste Teilaufgabe einen Punkt. Bei Lückentexten gibt es für jede richtig gefüllte Lücke einen Punkt. Bei Rechtschreibfehlern ziehe dir für jeden Fehler einen halben Punkt ab.
Beachte auch die weiteren Bewertungshinweise.

#### 1 Reading comprehension: famous immigrants

I.

A: was born – B: working for a make-up artist – C: to Los Angeles – D: make-up for Hollywood – E: lipgloss

II.

1. right – 2. wrong – 3. right – 4. right – 5. wrong – 6. wrong – 7. right – 8. wrong – 9. right – 10. right

III.

1. any/much money – 2. in some films – 3. he was great/handsome – 4. with his fans/with chaos – 5. broke windows/caused chaos

#### 2 Vocabulary: arriving at Ellis Island

1. essentially – 2. minority – 3. celebrities – 4. disappear – 5. Meanwhile – 6. reluctant – 7. employees – 8. evoked – 9. forced – 10. enhanced

#### 3 Vocabulary: How did they feel?

1. isolated – 2. anxious – 3. gloomy – 4. exhausted – 5. relieved

#### 4 Grammar: gerund constructions

1. on starting – 2. to meeting – 3. of traveling – 4. about finding – 5. spending

#### 5 Grammar: questions

1. can't we? – 2. will they? – 3. doesn't he? – 4. hasn't she? – 5. haven't they?

#### 6 Grammar: comparison of adjectives

1. more difficult – 2. friendlier – 3. more exciting – 4. worse – 5. most precious

#### 7 Text production: audio guide

Korrigiere deinen Text oder lasse ihn von jemandem korrigieren und verteile bis zu 10 Punkte (credits = cr.) für jeden Bereich anhand der folgenden Kriterien:
Form:
9–10 cr.: Thema wird genannt, Text ist in sinnvolle Abschnitte eingeteilt, im ersten Abschnitt werden die wichtigen Fragen (Wer? Was? Wann? Wo? Warum?) beantwortet, durchgehender roter Faden erkennbar, persönliche Haltung erkennbar, Ton ist für Leser passend gewählt
7–8 cr.: Thema nur angerissen, Abschnitte fehlen manchmal, der Einstieg ist langweilig, einzelne Fragen bleiben unbeantwortet, ab und zu fehlen Übergänge
5–6 cr.: Thema ist nur ungenau genannt, einige Fragen werden nicht beantwortet, Abschnitte fehlen, Zusammenhänge sind nicht immer verständlich
3–4 cr.:Thema bleibt unklar, im ersten Abschnitt werden nur einzelne Fragen beantwortet, Zusammenhänge fehlen oft, persönliche Haltung nur selten erkennbar
1–2 cr.: keine Absätze, im ersten Abschnitt werden wichtige Fragen nicht beantwortet, kein roter Faden erkennbar, keine persönliche Haltung erkennbar, Ton trifft Anlass nicht
Inhalt:
9–10 cr.: Informationen sind gezielt für eine allgemeine Information über den Ort ausgewählt, Unnötiges ist weggelassen (z. B. zu viele Details), die Quellen sind einbezogen, spannende und lebendige Einzelheiten sind ergänzt, Gedankengang ist schlüssig und nachvollziehbar
7–8 cr.: einzelne Informationen fehlen, einzelne unnötige Details sind übernommen, Gedankengang ist an einzelnen Stellen unklar
5–6 cr.: im Großen und Ganzen sind die wichtigen Informationen vorhanden, der Gedankengang ist bis auf einige Stellen klar, Informationen sind manchmal oberflächlich dargestellt, einzelne Wiederholungen treten auf
3–4 cr.: Informationen fehlen oder sind an einzelnen Stellen falsch, einzelne Quellen sind nicht bearbeitet, nur pauschale Behauptungen ohne interessante Ausschmückungen sind vorhanden, Informationen werden aneinandergereiht
1–2 cr.: Informationen sind falsch übernommen, zu viele Details sind übernommen, Informationen sind nur pauschal und oberflächlich wiedergegeben, Wiederholungen treten auf, Gedankengang ist wirr
Sprache:
9–10 cr.: sprachlich fehlerfrei, ganz selten Rechtschreibfehler, abwechslungsreiche Formulierungen, keine Wortwiederholungen, Sätze sind mit Nebensätzen gebildet und hängen zusammen
7–8 cr.: einzelne Fehler in Wortschatz oder Grammatik (z. B. tenses), manchmal werden Wörter wiederholt, einzelne Sätze sind nicht verknüpft
5–6 cr.: einfache Sätze ohne Nebensätze, häufige Fehler in Wortschatz und Grammatik (v.a. *tenses*, Satzbau), nur ganz selten sind Sätze verknüpft
3–4 cr.: an einzelnen Stellen ist der Text unverständlich, weil falsche oder deutsche Wörter verwendet werden oder die Grammatik völlig falsch verwendet ist
1–2 cr.: Text ist über weite Strecken unverständlich, falsche oder deutsche Wörter werden verwendet, Grammatik wird (fast) durchgehend falsch verwendet

Example

Ellis Island – the "Isle of Tears". This was the name which was given to the little island right on the border of New York. But who were the people who thought so badly about this place? And why?
It was the immigrants who came to the USA who renamed the place. In the 19th century many thousands of Europeans came to the USA to find a better life. They traveled on ships across the Atlantic, and they arrived in New York. Before they were allowed to immigrate, they had to pass the buildings of Ellis Island, and this experience was not too good for many of them. First they had to wait for a long time – you can see the line of

people waiting in the picture, with all their bags and suitcases. Just imagine you have to carry everything you own with you! In the other picture you can see how awful it must have been to walk around with your family and all your belongings! And of course they were nervous and frightened, because they didn't know what would happen to them. Just look at the faces of the group of people in the other picture! Most of the immigrants had completely given up their old life, but at Ellis Island some of them had to go back. If you look at these pictures, you can see the reason: there were very strict medical examinations – and those who showed signs of illness were just sent home again. How frustrating that must have been! And how relieved those must have been who were allowed to start their new lives!

## Lösungen zur Klassenarbeit Christmas in New York – Test 2

### Seite 61

Soweit nicht anders angegeben, gib dir für jede richtig gelöste Teilaufgabe einen Punkt. Bei Lückentexten gibt es für jede richtig gefüllte Lücke einen Punkt. Bei Rechtschreibfehlern ziehe dir für jeden Fehler einen halben Punkt ab.
Beachte auch die weiteren Bewertungshinweise.

#### 1 Reading comprehension: Christmas shopping

I.
1. 45 – 2. 798 – 3. most famous – 4. 1858 – 5. red star – 6. 11 – 7. 1912 – 8. 3000 – 9. 1927 – 10. 1947 – 11. 1994

II.
1. wrong – 2. right – 3. wrong

III.
1. People go to Tiffany's to buy diamonds or rings.
2. Tiffany's is located on 5th Avenue.
3. The business was founded in 1837.
4. On the first day Tiffany's made only about 5 dollars.
5. Many women love "Breakfast at Tiffany's".
6. Tiffany's was also famous for the blue boxes which you got when you bought something.

#### 2 Vocabulary: Christmas shopping

1. appealing – 2. precious – 3. crowded – 4. eventually – 5. expectations – 6. fed – 7. concepts – 8. walk around – 9. contain – 10. raise

#### 3 Vocabulary: American or British English?

1. cab – 2. French fries – 3. cookies – 4. cell phone – 5. apartment

#### 4 Grammar: gerund constructions

1. in going – 2. of visiting – 3. about spending – 4. to take – 5. to drink

#### 5 Grammar: questions

1. can't we? – 2. will they? – 3. don't they? – 4. can I? – 5. don't you?

#### 6 Grammar: comparison of adjectives

1. most amazing – 2. taller – 3. better – 4. more interesting – 5. as exciting

#### 7 Text production: online chat (mediation)

Korrigiere deinen Text oder lasse ihn von jemandem korrigieren und verteile bis zu 10 Punkte (credits = cr.) für jeden Bereich anhand der folgenden Kriterien:
Form:
9–10 cr.: Anknüpfung an vorige Äußerung ist vorhanden, im ersten Satz wird Bezug auf bereits Gesagtes bzw. die Frage genommen; Text ist weitgehend in sinnvolle Abschnitte gegliedert, durchgehend ist ein roter Faden erkennbar, durchgehend wird der Adressat angesprochen, Ton ist passend
7–8 cr.: im ersten Satz fehlt eine passende Anknüpfung, der Chat-Beitrag hört abrupt auf, ansonsten ist der Text in Abschnitte gegliedert, ein roter Faden ist erkennbar, der Adressat wird angesprochen
5–6 cr.: der Text beginnt zusammenhanglos mit einer Information, der Adressat wird kaum angesprochen, Absätze fehlen, meistens sind die Zusammenhänge unklar
3–4 cr.: es werden keine Absätze gebildet, der Adressat wird kaum angesprochen, unterschiedliche Informationen stehen zusammenhanglos nebeneinander
1–2 cr.: keine Absätze vorhanden, keine direkte Anrede an den Adressaten erkennbar
Inhalt:
9–10 cr.: die gefragten Informationen sind sinnvoll ausgewählt und mit eigenen Ideen ausgebaut, die Informationen sind korrekt und schlüssig, der Adressat wird persönlich angesprochen, die eigene Haltung des Schreibers wird deutlich
7–8 cr.: die gefragten Aspekte sind genannt, ohne dass darauf näher eingegangen wird, die Aussagen sind weitgehend persönlich und originell, der Adressat wird meistens angesprochen
5–6 cr.: im Großen und Ganzen sind die wichtigen Informationen vorhanden, der Gedankengang ist bis auf einige Stellen klar, die Aussagen sind streckenweise oberflächlich und sehr pauschal, einzelne Wiederholungen treten auf
3–4 cr.: Informationen fehlen oder sind an einzelnen Stellen falsch, nur pauschale Behauptungen ohne interessante Ausschmückungen sind vorhanden, Informationen werden aneinandergereiht, kein Adressatenbezug erkennbar
1–2 cr.: Informationen sind falsch oder fehlen ganz, Aussagen sind nur pauschal und oberflächlich, Wiederholungen treten auf, Gedankengang ist wirr, Adressatenbezug fehlt ganz
Sprache:
9–10 cr.: sprachlich fehlerfrei, ganz selten Rechtschreibfehler, abwechslungsreiche Formulierungen, keine Wortwiederholungen, Sätze sind mit Nebensätzen gebildet und hängen zusammen
7–8 cr.: einzelne Fehler in Wortschatz oder Grammatik (z. B. *tenses*), manchmal werden Wörter wiederholt, einzelne Sätze sind nicht verknüpft
5–6 cr.: einfache Sätze ohne Nebensätze, häufige Fehler in Wortschatz und Grammatik (v. a. *tenses*, Satzbau), nur ganz selten sind Sätze verknüpft
3–4 cr.: an einzelnen Stellen ist der Text unverständlich, weil falsche oder deutsche Wörter verwendet werden oder die Grammatik völlig falsch verwendet ist

1–2 cr.: Text ist über weite Strecken unverständlich, falsche oder deutsche Wörter werden verwendet, Grammatik wird (fast) durchgehend falsch verwendet.

Example

... You're right, it's great that you will be here in the days before Christmas! And of course we will visit one of the Christmas markets. There are different ones, you know. There are really huge and famous ones like in Nuremberg, but there are also smaller ones. And there is one right next to our house! It takes place in the town center, on the market square, so there are also many shops around. Most of the stalls sell only drinks, and the drinks are usually alcoholic (but at least they'll be warm). Some stalls sell Christmas decorations. I'm not sure if they will impress you – the American decorations flash a lot more and are brighter than ours. There are things to see, too, like real sheep next to the baby Jesus, or "real" angels. If we go on Sunday, we can even meet Santa Claus, but I guess we're too old to have fun there. But we will certainly walk around, look at the stalls, get something to drink and maybe listen to the music. Yes, there's a live concert, too! I bet you don't have that in your Christmas markets!

## Theme 4: Colorado

### Seite 65

#### 1 German – English

1. assume – 2. independence – 3. introduction – 4. inconsiderate – 5. unacceptable – 6. condition – 7. outrageous – 8. irresponsible

#### 2 The infinitive perfect

1. should have brought – 2. should have listened – 3. should have taught

#### 3 Conditional clauses

1. would not have met – 2. came – 3. stays – 4. lived – 5. had not been alone – 6. will invite

#### 4 Adverbs of degree

1. After a wilderness therapy many teenagers feel terribly sorry about their life.
2. When they have to spend one night alone in the wilderness, they are extremely frightened.
3. But after the therapy most of them try awfully hard to finish school and find a job.

#### 5 The infintive after question words

1. Rachel didn't know where to stay during the wilderness therapy.
2. The guides always wonder what to tell the teenagers about their stay in the wilderness.
3. James wasn't sure how to put up his tent.
4. James wondered where he could put his clothes.
5. The teenagers' parents always wonder what they should say to their children when they meet again after the camp.
6. After the camp, the teenagers usually don't ask how they could cope with difficulties at school.

#### 6 Stative verbs

You had to circle:
hated – seemed – saw + were sitting – think – am thinking

#### 7 Dylan's experiences

You had to circle:
lonely – taking drugs – in the streets – stole things – nearly nothing – helpless – he wouldn't survive – much stronger – will be able to cope with all his problems

#### 8 The Rocky Mountain Wilderness Therapy

You had to tick off:
1. drugs, the police, alcohol – 2. teenagers, lost in a city – 3. work together, be able to cope with challenges on their own, cook, put up tents, learn how to protect themselves from wild animals, walk every day – 4 . something to eat and drink, something to call for help – 5. people with experience in medical support, people with experience in therapies, people who know how to cope with challenges in nature

#### 9 Magazine Page

Example:

**Going wild – and back again**

Living in the streets, taking drugs – that was James's life, a life that had ended before it had really begun. But he was lucky: he had the chance to start all over again, when he was sent to a wilderness therapy.
For weeks he lived in the wilderness, together with other teenagers and supported by therapists.
Coping with the challenges of everyday life, facing the dangers of the wilderness and working together with others was a new experience for James. Never before had he been on a mountain, and never before had he been sitting round a campfire and listening to somebody playing the guitar. All this made him stronger, he says. The most important experience, however, was the trip into the wild on his own, with nothing but the most basic things he needed to survive for three days.
When he came back, he knew: He had managed all this, so he would manage all other challenges, too. However, there is still a rest of doubt: what about his former friends? Will they lead him back onto the old streets? And will he then be strong enough to say "no" again? The only thing that is sure is that he won't get a second chance ...

### 10 Letter to the editor

Dear Sir,
I just read the article about James's experiences during the wilderness therapy. This teenager says that the therapy is an opportunity for most young people, but it is also very expensive. I agree with this opinion.
The teenagers who take part in wilderness therapies often come from bigger cities. They have learned to cope with difficulties in an anonymous and chaotic place, and for them the experience of the loneliness of nature certainly is something special. But what will happen when they get back into the city again? They will meet their old friends, they will see the old streets, they will be back in their old life again. Not all teenagers will be strong enough to say "no" to their old life after only some weeks in a different place.
So is it really necessary to spend so much money on therapies which are not completely successful? I think it would be better if communities spent their money on programs in the cities to get the teenagers back to a normal life. This would not only help the few who are chosen for the wilderness, but all the others, too. And maybe these programs could help some teenagers even before they get into trouble.
All in all, every teenager should be given support, not only some of them.
Henry O'Donnell, Longfield

## Lösungen zur Klassenarbeit Going wild – Test 1

### Seite 71

Soweit nicht anders angegeben, gib dir für jede richtig gelöste Teilaufgabe einen Punkt. Bei Lückentexten gibt es für jede richtig gefüllte Lücke einen Punkt. Bei Rechtschreibfehlern ziehe dir für jeden Fehler einen halben Punkt ab.
Beachte auch die weiteren Bewertungshinweise.

### 1 Listening comprehension: The Black Canyon of the Gunnison Park

I.
You had to circle:
1. sometimes – 2. Knowing that there are always other people not too far away – 3. steep – 4. hold onto their children

II.
You had to tick off:
know the rules – take care of your food – find a locker for your food – put your tobacco into a locker – not leave any toothpaste lying around in the camp – tidy up after dinner – throw away all the food which you have not eaten

III.
campsite South: 90 sites – electricity – booking; campsites North and East: 15 sites – no electricity – no booking

IV.
1. (groups of) teenagers – 2. the animals – 3. frightened/aggressive

### 2 Vocabulary: teenagers' problems

1. lovesick – 2. addicted – 3. suffer – 4. hang out – 5. arguments – 6. own – 7. the laundry – 8. deal

### 3 Grammar: the perfect infinitive

1. have left – 2. have carried – 3. have tried

### 4 Grammar: the conditional

1. be – 2. wouldn't have happened – 3. were – 4. ask – 5. hadn't spent – 6. became – 7. would look – 8. didn't work

### 5 Grammar: adverbs of degree

1. If you meet a bear in the National Park, you must be extremely careful.
2. Don't run away. Just move absolutely slowly!
3. If you are attacked by a bear, you can be seriously injured.

### 6 Grammar: the infinitive after question words

1. Many tourists don't know where to get information about the trails through the National Park.
2. So they wonder where they can find the important rules of behaviour for the National Park.
3. If something happens, they often don't know who they can ask for help.
4. But the rangers usually know how to find the hikers after an accident.

### 7 Grammar: stative verbs

1. sounded – 2. Do you think – 3. was walking – 4. hate

### 8 Text production: article for a magazine (mediation)

Korrigiere deinen Text oder lasse ihn von jemandem korrigieren und verteile bis zu 10 Punkte (credits = cr.) für jeden Bereich anhand der folgenden Kriterien:
Form:
9–10 cr.: Überschrift ist kurz und treffend, Text ist in Abschnitte eingeteilt, im ersten Abschnitt wird die Neugier des Lesers geweckt und das Thema genannt, durchgehender roter Faden erkennbar, persönliche Haltung erkennbar, Ton ist für Leser passend gewählt
7–8 cr.: Überschrift ist sehr lang, Abschnitte fehlen manchmal, der Einstieg ist langweilig, einzelne Fragen bleiben unbeantwortet, ab und zu fehlen Übergänge
5–6 cr.: Überschrift besteht aus ganzem Satz und passt nicht genau zum Thema, einige Fragen werden nicht beantwortet, Abschnitte fehlen, Zusammenhänge sind nicht immer verständlich
3–4 cr.: keine oder unpassende Überschrift, im ersten Abschnitt werden nur einzelne Fragen beantwortet, Zusammenhänge fehlen oft, persönliche Haltung nur selten erkennbar
1–2 cr.: keine oder unpassende Überschrift, keine Absätze, im ersten Abschnitt wird das Thema nicht genannt, kein roter Faden erkennbar, keine persönliche Haltung erkennbar, Ton trifft Anlass nicht

Inhalt:
9–10 cr.: Informationen sind gezielt für einen allgemeinen Artikel ausgewählt, Unnötiges ist weggelassen (z. B. Namen), alle Quellen sind einbezogen, spannende und lebendige Einzelheiten sind ergänzt, Gedankengang ist schlüssig und nachvollziehbar
7–8 cr.: einzelne Informationen fehlen, einzelne unnötige Details sind übernommen, Gedankengang ist an einzelnen Stellen unklar
5–6 cr.: im Großen und Ganzen sind die wichtigen Informationen vorhanden, der Gedankengang ist bis auf einige Stellen klar, Informationen sind manchmal oberflächlich dargestellt, einzelne Wiederholungen treten auf
3–4 cr.: Informationen fehlen oder sind an einzelnen Stellen falsch, einzelne Quellen sind nicht bearbeitet, nur pauschale Behauptungen ohne interessante Ausschmückungen sind vorhanden, Informationen werden aneinandergereiht
1–2 cr.: Informationen sind falsch übernommen, zu viele Details sind übernommen, Informationen sind nur pauschal und oberflächlich wiedergegeben, Wiederholungen treten auf, Gedankengang ist wirr
Sprache:
9–10 cr.: sprachlich fehlerfrei, ganz selten Rechtschreibfehler, abwechslungsreiche Formulierungen, keine Wortwiederholungen, Sätze sind mit Nebensätzen gebildet und hängen zusammen
7–8 cr.: einzelne Fehler in Wortschatz oder Grammatik (z. B. *tenses*), manchmal werden Wörter wiederholt, einzelne Sätze sind nicht verknüpft
5–6 cr.: einfache Sätze ohne Nebensätze, häufige Fehler in Wortschatz und Grammatik (v. a. *tenses*, Satzbau), nur ganz selten sind Sätze verknüpft
3–4 cr.: an einzelnen Stellen ist der Text unverständlich, weil falsche oder deutsche Wörter verwendet werden oder die Grammatik völlig falsch verwendet ist
1–2 cr.: Text ist über weite Strecken unverständlich, falsche oder deutsche Wörter werden verwendet, Grammatik wird (fast) durchgehend falsch verwendet

Example

**The Not-So-Rocky Mountains in Bavaria**

Great Sand Dunes, Mesa Verde, Rocky Mountains – in the USA there are many famous and spectacular national parks. Are there any beautiful national parks in Germany? Yes, there are. And one of the most beautiful ones is the Bavarian Forest National Park in the east of Bavaria.
It is not only very idyllic with many woods and lakes, and also little villages right next to it. It was also the first national park in Germany. If you go there, you will be surprised about the wilderness in the middle of Europe – there are thousands of square metres of tall trees, and there are also mountains from where you have a wonderful view over the whole area.
It's the ideal place to go hiking, or you can go cycling. (And for the golden oldies: you can even explore the forest on an electric bike!) You might even meet horseback riders!
So if you want to spend some time far away from people and you don't want to stay in the USA – why not visit Germany and the wild old forest?

# Lösungen zur Klassenarbeit Protecting the environment – Test 2

## Seite 76

Soweit nicht anders angegeben, gib dir für jede richtig gelöste Teilaufgabe einen Punkt. Bei Lückentexten gibt es für jede richtig gefüllte Lücke einen Punkt. Bei Rechtschreibfehlern ziehe dir für jeden Fehler einen halben Punkt ab.
Beachte auch die weiteren Bewertungshinweise.

### 1 Reading comprehension: protest against fracking

I.
1. jobs – 2. money – 3. waste of resources – 4. listen – 5. the land – 6. the farms – 7. lives – 8. water – 9. air – 10. people – 11. animals – 12. gas – 13. destroyed

II.
You had to tick off:
organizing demonstrations – talking to the media – preventing the trucks from driving to the site

III.
1. not allow the (protest group's) activities – 2. understands the fears of the protesters – 3. not be taken too seriously/be ignored – 4. doesn't take the protest seriously

### 2 Vocabulary: protecting the environment

1. in favour of – 2. doubt – 3. activist group – 4. groundwater – 5. contaminated – 6. toxic – 7. extracted – 8. turned down

### 3 Grammar: the perfect infinitive

1. have organized – 2. have listened – 3. have known

### 4 Grammar: the conditional

1. don't protest – 2. would have stayed – 3. would have been – 4. will even take – 5. were – 6. is – 7. had known – 8. will be destroyed

### 5 Grammar: adverbs of degree

1. The fracking companies say that the risks of fracking are highly exaggerated.
2. Protest groups, however, think that it would be dangerously wrong not to take the risks seriously.
3. The movie "Gasland" shows that the risks are extremely high.

### 6 Grammar: the infinitive after question words

1. When Carl Johnson decided to join the protest group, he didn't know at first where to meet the others.
2. The other members of the group asked him what they should write onto the posters.
3. And they asked him what they should bring for the next meeting.
4. Soon Carl Johnson found out how to organize everything.

### 7 Grammar: stative verbs

1. likes – 2. also thinks – 3. is thinking – 4. were blocking

### 8 Text production: letter to the editor

Korrigiere deinen Text oder lasse ihn von jemandem korrigieren und verteile bis zu 10 Punkte (credits = cr.) für jeden Bereich anhand der folgenden Kriterien:
Form:
9–10 cr.: Anrede und Einleitung sind formal einwandfrei, im ersten Abschnitt wird deutlich, auf welchen Artikel und welche Aussage sich der Brief bezieht, der Grund für den Brief wird genannt, die Gründe sind sinnvoll und ausführlich erläutert, die Meinung ist deutlich, ein durchgehender roter Faden ist erkennbar, der Ton ist unpersönlich und formal gelungen, der Brief endet mit einer klaren Aussage und der Unterschrift
7–8 cr.: einzelne Teile eines Leserbriefs fehlen, in der Einleitung wird der Artikel genannt, die Aussage ist aber nur undeutlich, die Gründe sind sinnvoll, aber nur wenig erläutert, die Meinung ist deutlich, an einzelnen Stellen ist der rote Faden nicht erkennbar
5–6 cr.: mehrere Teile eines Leserbriefs fehlen, in der Einleitung werden Artikel und Aussage undeutlich genannt, die Gründe sind teils sinnvoll und gut erläutert, teils unlogisch oder zu kurz genannt, die Meinung ist deutlich, an mehreren Stellen ist der rote Faden nicht erkennbar, der Ton ist nicht immer formal und unpersönlich gelungen
3–4 cr.: mehrere Teile des Leserbriefs fehlen oder sind falsch ausgeführt, in der Einleitung fehlt der Bezug zum Artikel, die Gründe sind kaum überzeugend erklärt, Zusammenhänge fehlen oft, die persönliche Haltung ist nur selten erkennbar
1–2 cr.: die Teile des Leserbriefs sind nicht erkennbar, im ersten Abschnitt wird kein Bezug auf den Artikel genommen, die Gründe sind unsinnig und nicht erklärt, kein roter Faden erkennbar, keine persönliche Haltung erkennbar, Ton ist nicht formal und unpersönlich
Inhalt:
9–10 cr.: Informationen sind gezielt für einen Leserbrief zu einem Zeitungsartikel ausgewählt, die Aussage des Artikels wird klar genannt, die Gründe sind wichtig und ausführlich erklärt, die Aussage am Schluss des Leserbriefs ist überzeugend und ergibt sich aus den Gründen, der Gedankengang ist schlüssig und nachvollziehbar
7–8 cr.: einzelne Informationen sind nicht schlüssig ausgewählt, einzelne unnötige Details sind ausgeführt, während wichtige Punkte nicht berücksichtigt sind, die Aussage am Schluss des Leserbriefs ist immer noch überzeugend, der Gedankengang ist an einzelnen Stellen unklar
5–6 cr.: im Großen und Ganzen wird Bezug auf den Artikel genommen, die Gründe sind brauchbar ausgewählt und knapp erklärt, die eigene Meinung ist genannt, der Gedankengang ist bis auf einige Stellen klar, einzelne Wiederholungen treten auf
3–4 cr.: der Bezug auf den Zeitungsartikel ist falsch oder fehlt ganz, die Gründe sind nur ganz schwach und kaum erklärt, meistens nur mit pauschalen Behauptungen ausgeführt, eigene Meinung und Aussage am Schluss bleiben unklar, die einzelnen Punkte sind nur aneinandergereiht
1–2 cr.: der Bezug zum Zeitungsartikel ist falsch wiedergegeben, die Gründe sind ganz schwach und nicht sinnvoll erklärt, Wiederholungen treten auf, der Gedankengang ist wirr, die eigene Meinung und eine Aussage am Schluss fehlen ganz
Sprache:
9–10 cr.: sprachlich fehlerfrei, ganz selten Rechtschreibfehler, abwechslungsreiche Formulierungen, keine Wortwiederholungen, Sätze sind mit Nebensätzen gebildet und hängen zusammen
7–8 cr.: einzelne Fehler in Wortschatz oder Grammatik (z. B. *tenses*), manchmal werden Wörter wiederholt, einzelne Sätze sind nicht verknüpft
5–6 cr.: einfache Sätze ohne Nebensätze, häufige Fehler in Wortschatz und Grammatik (v. a. *tenses*, Satzbau), nur ganz selten sind Sätze verknüpft
3–4 cr.: an einzelnen Stellen ist der Text unverständlich, weil falsche oder deutsche Wörter verwendet werden oder die Grammatik völlig falsch verwendet ist
1–2 cr.: Text ist über weite Strecken unverständlich, falsche oder deutsche Wörter werden verwendet, Grammatik wird (fast) durchgehend falsch verwendet

Example
Sir,
I have read your article about the new fracking site near Longfield. It says that there is a protest group who also want to organize illegal activities against these plans. Personally, I doubt that these activities will be successful.
As a supporter of a protest group against fracking I am well aware of the risks and dangers of fracking. These dangers must not be ignored, because the consequences of any accident at a fracking site will affect the lives of all people, animals and plants in the area.
But even though I strongly believe that fracking sites should not be opened irresponsibly, I'm convinced that illegal activities are the wrong way to make people aware of the dangers. If illegal methods to protest are used, many people will be angry about the protesters themselves, and not about the fracking companies.
What matters in the end is that as many people as possible will support the protest group, so that new sites will not be opened.
Jimmy Connor

# Theme 5: California

## Seite 81

### 1 Jumbled letters

1. contest – 2. heartbreaking – 3. documentary – 4. self-conscious – 5. jeopardize – 6. wealthy

### 2 Adjectives and adverbs

1. lonely – 2. quickly – 3. important – 4. fantastic – 5. really happy

### 3 The infinitive without *to*

1. go – 2. to stay – 3. cry – 4. cry – 5. to leave – to find

### 4 Silicon Valley

1. California – 2. Sunnyvale – 3. industrial area – 4. computer technologies – 5. international – 6. toxic chemicals – 7. cleaning the grounds – 8. have always done

### 5 The actress
You had to tick off:
1. right – 2. wrong – 3. wrong – 4. right – 5. right – 6. wrong – 7. right – 8. right – 9. wrong

### 6 Cartoon
Example:
The cartoon shows the problem that in USA little girls are treated like grown-up women just to become famous.
In the picture you can see two women standing next to a catwalk at a show. On the stage there is a little girl, but she is wearing the clothes of a grown-up woman. One woman talks to the other about the girl, but she doesn't realize that they are talking about a girl. She thinks they are talking about a woman.
In the USA you can often see girls who are dressed up like stars, for example at beauty pageants. Mostly they are there together with their mothers, and they make their daughters wear inappropriate dresses or make-up, just because they think that their child should be a star. This attitude of some mothers in the USA is criticized in the cartoon.

### 7 Comment
Example:
In California there are many Hispanics, and most of them live in very bad conditions. Now some people want to organize a center for Hispanic immigrants in Los Angeles to support them.
The immigrants have many problems in California. They often get jobs in which they have to work very hard and in which they are treated badly, like on the fields or in houses. They don't earn much money, so they work for many hours a day. And they can't defend themselves. Therefore it is a good idea to establish a center in which they can get help.
Moreover, if there is a center like that, the immigrants get in touch with other people and also with Americans. So they will learn how to behave and how to lead a normal life in California. Maybe they will find other immigrants and share their experiences, or they might make friends with people who have lived in Los Angeles for a longer time and who can help them.
So I think it is a great idea to establish this center, and it is great that there are people who try to organize support for the Hispanic immigrants.

# Lösungen zur Klassenarbeit Hispanics in California – Test 1

## Seite 86

Soweit nicht anders angegeben, gib dir für jede richtig gelöste Teilaufgabe einen Punkt. Bei Lückentexten gibt es für jede richtig gefüllte Lücke einen Punkt. Bei Rechtschreibfehlern ziehe dir für jeden Fehler einen halben Punkt ab.
Beachte auch die weiteren Bewertungshinweise.

### 1 Listening comprehension: Miguel
I.
You had to tick off:
1. in California – 2. quite often – 3. in Mexico – 4. with his mother and his brothers and sisters – 5. she wanted a better life for her children – 6. was only ten years old – 7. to go to school

II.
1. (strawberry) farm – 2. hard/bad – 3. help/support – 4. working hours – 5. hot – 6. boxes/containers – 7. hated/didn't like

III.
1. wrong – 2. right – 3. right – 4. wrong – 5. right – 6. wrong

### 2 Vocabulary: Hispanics in California
1. border – 2. fences – 3. self-conscious – 4. shy – 5. apart – 6. keep up – 7. income – 8. violated – 9. ruin – 10. enter

### 3 Grammar: adjectives and adverbs
1. relaxed – 2. talk – 3. different – 4. higher – 5. extremely, disappointed – 6. sad – 7. hard

### 4 Grammar: the infinitive with and without *to*
1. talk – 2. speak – 3. to use – 4. work – 5. to go – 6. go

### 5 Grammar: mixed tenses
1. had not known – 2. had met – 3. have reacted – 4. has learned – 5. won't talk – 6. is going to tell

### 6 Text production: cartoon
Korrigiere deinen Text oder lasse ihn von jemandem korrigieren und verteile bis zu 10 Punkte (credits = cr.) für jeden Bereich anhand der folgenden Kriterien:
Form:
9–10 cr.: Text ist in Abschnitte eingeteilt, im ersten Abschnitt wird das Thema genannt, die Beschreibung und die Erklärung sind sauber getrennt; durchgehender roter Faden erkennbar, am Ende wird die Aussage des Cartoons genannt
7–8 cr.: Abschnitte fehlen manchmal, der Einstieg ist nur oberflächlich, die Beschreibung ist unvollständig, die Erklärung fehlt, ab und zu fehlen Übergänge, die Aussage des Cartoons ist nur oberflächlich angerissen
5–6 cr.: Thema ist nicht genau oder unpassend genannt, einige unwichtige Einzelheiten des Cartoons sind genannt, wichtige Elemente fehlen, Erklärungen sind pauschal oder ungenau, Zusammenhänge sind nicht immer verständlich, die Aussage ist nur unvollständig oder nicht ganz passend
3–4 cr.: Thema fehlt oder ist falsch angegeben, Beschreibung des Cartoons nur in groben Zügen, mit einzelnen falschen Aussagen,

Erklärungen fehlen, Aussage nur unvollständig wiedergegeben, kaum Zusammenhänge erkennbar
1–2 cr.: Thema wird falsch oder gar nicht genannt, Beschreibung trifft Cartoon nicht, Erklärungen werden nicht oder falsch gegeben, Aussage fehlt ganz oder trifft den Cartoon gar nicht, kein roter Faden erkennbar
Inhalt:
9–10 cr.: Cartoon wird zielstrebig und genau beschrieben, Unnötiges ist weggelassen, Erklärungen sind schlüssig, Aussage trifft Kern des Cartoons, Gedankengang ist schlüssig und nachvollziehbar
7–8 cr.: einzelne Informationen fehlen, einzelne unnötige Details sind übernommen, Gedankengang ist an einzelnen Stellen unklar
5–6 cr.: im Großen und Ganzen sind die wichtigen Informationen vorhanden, der Gedankengang ist bis auf einige Stellen klar, Informationen sind manchmal oberflächlich dargestellt, einzelne Wiederholungen treten auf
3–4 cr.: Informationen fehlen oder sind an einzelnen Stellen falsch, nur pauschale Behauptungen sind vorhanden, Informationen werden aneinandergereiht
1–2 cr.: Informationen sind falsch übernommen, zu viele Details sind übernommen, Informationen sind nur pauschal und oberflächlich wiedergegeben, Wiederholungen treten auf, Gedankengang ist wirr
Sprache:
9–10 cr.: sprachlich fehlerfrei, ganz selten Rechtschreibfehler, abwechslungsreiche Formulierungen, keine Wortwiederholungen, Sätze sind mit Nebensätzen gebildet und hängen zusammen
7–8 cr.: einzelne Fehler in Wortschatz oder Grammatik (z. B. *tenses*), manchmal werden Wörter wiederholt, einzelne Sätze sind nicht verknüpft
5–6 cr.: einfache Sätze ohne Nebensätze, häufige Fehler in Wortschatz und Grammatik (v. a. *tenses*, Satzbau), nur ganz selten sind Sätze verknüpft
3–4 cr.: an einzelnen Stellen ist der Text unverständlich, weil falsche oder deutsche Wörter verwendet werden oder die Grammatik völlig falsch verwendet ist
1–2 cr.: Text ist über weite Strecken unverständlich, falsche oder deutsche Wörter werden verwendet, Grammatik wird (fast) durchgehend falsch verwendet

Example
The cartoon shows the attitude of many Americans towards Hispanic immigrants.
In the picture you can see two white Americans sitting in a room. In the background of the room there are objects and decorations which show that these people must be quite wealthy. There are also three Hispanic girls in the room wearing servants' dresses. They are doing the work that must be done in a household. The white couple thinks that immigration should be stopped, because they are afraid that the Hispanic immigrants will take away the white people's jobs.
In the USA, especially in California, there are many Hispanic immigrants. Most of them work as cheap workers in households or on farms, and they do the jobs which the white Americans usually don't want to do. Many Americans don't realize that without these immigrants they would have to do these jobs themselves, but they nevertheless think that there are too many immigrants.
So the cartoon criticizes this attitude of many white Americans by showing how stupid it is.

# Lösungen zur Klassenarbeit Hollywood – Test 2

## Seite 90

Soweit nicht anders angegeben, gib dir für jede richtig gelöste Teilaufgabe einen Punkt. Bei Lückentexten gibt es für jede richtig gefüllte Lücke einen Punkt. Bei Rechtschreibfehlern ziehe dir für jeden Fehler einen halben Punkt ab.
Beachte auch die weiteren Bewertungshinweise.

### 1 Reading comprehension: child stars now and then

I.
1. right – 2. wrong – 3. right – 4. wrong – 5. right – 6. wrong – 7. wrong

II.
1. Hollywood – 2. loved dancing/wanted to dance – 3. (film) director – 4. a role – 5. six – 6. President – 7. arguments – 8. political

III.
You had to tick off: depressions – loneliness – illegal activities – addiction to alcohol – no experience of a "normal life"

### 2 Vocabulary: film stars

1. shot – 2. rehearse – 3. vain – 4. encourage – 5. harmful – 6. proof – 7. acting – 8. increases – 9. ashamed – 10. steady

### 3 Grammar: adjectives and adverbs

1. sad – 2. wonderful – 3. disappointed – 4. harder – 5. terribly, bad – 6. well – 7. happy

### 4 Grammar: the infinitive with and without *to*

1. walk – 2. eat – 3. to do – 4. give – 5. shout – 6. leave

### 5 Grammar: mixed tenses

1. had worked – 2. was thinking – 3. suggested – 4. developed – 5. will still enjoy – 6. had known

### 6 Text production: comment

Korrigiere deinen Text oder lasse ihn von jemandem korrigieren und verteile bis zu 10 Punkte (credits = cr.) für jeden Bereich anhand der folgenden Kriterien:
Form:
9–10 cr.: im ersten Abschnitt wird deutlich, zu welchem Thema Stellung bezogen wird, Grund für den *comment* wird genannt, die Argumente sind sinnvoll und ausführlich erläutert, die Meinung ist deutlich, ein durchgehender roter Faden ist erkennbar
7–8 cr.: in der Einleitung wird das Thema nur undeutlich genannt, die Argumente sind sinnvoll, aber nur wenig erläutert, die Meinung ist deutlich, an einzelnen Stellen ist der rote Faden nicht erkennbar
5–6 cr.: in der Einleitung ist das Thema nur oberflächlich genannt, die Gründe sind teils sinnvoll und gut erläutert, teils unlogisch oder zu kurz genannt, die Meinung ist deutlich, an mehreren Stellen ist der rote Faden nicht erkennbar
3–4 cr.: in der Einleitung wird das Thema nicht deutlich, die Gründe sind kaum überzeugend erklärt, Zusammenhänge fehlen oft
1–2 cr.: im ersten Abschnitt wird das Thema gar nicht oder falsch genannt, die Gründe sind unsinnig und nicht erklärt, kein roter Faden erkennbar

Inhalt:
9–10 cr.: Informationen sind gezielt ausgewählt, die Gründe sind wichtig und ausführlich erklärt, die Meinung am Schluss ist überzeugend und ergibt sich aus den Gründen, der Gedankengang ist schlüssig und nachvollziehbar
7–8 cr.: einzelne Informationen sind nicht schlüssig ausgewählt, einzelne unnötige Details sind ausgeführt, während wichtige Punkte nicht berücksichtigt sind, die Meinung am Schluss ist immer noch überzeugend, der Gedankengang ist an einzelnen Stellen unklar
5–6 cr.: im Großen und Ganzen wird das Thema ordentlich dargestellt, die Gründe sind brauchbar ausgewählt und knapp erklärt, die eigene Meinung ist genannt, der Gedankengang ist bis auf einige Stellen klar, einzelne Wiederholungen treten auf
3–4 cr.: das Thema ist falsch oder nur oberflächlich verstanden, die Gründe sind nur ganz schwach und kaum erklärt, meistens nur mit pauschalen Behauptungen ausgeführt, eigene Meinung am Schluss bleibt unklar, die einzelnen Punkte sind nur aneinandergereiht
1–2 cr.: das Thema wird gar nicht genannt, die Gründe sind ganz schwach und nicht sinnvoll erklärt, Wiederholungen treten auf, der Gedankengang ist wirr, die eigene Meinung am Schluss fehlt ganz
Sprache:
9–10 cr.: sprachlich fehlerfrei, ganz selten Rechtschreibfehler, abwechslungsreiche Formulierungen, keine Wortwiederholungen, Sätze sind mit Nebensätzen gebildet und hängen zusammen
7–8 cr.: einzelne Fehler in Wortschatz oder Grammatik (z. B.: *tenses*), manchmal werden Wörter wiederholt, einzelne Sätze sind nicht verknüpft
5–6 cr.: einfache Sätze ohne Nebensätze, häufige Fehler in Wortschatz und Grammatik (v. a. *tenses*, Satzbau), nur ganz selten sind Sätze verknüpft
3–4 cr.: an einzelnen Stellen ist der Text unverständlich, weil falsche oder deutsche Wörter verwendet werden oder die Grammatik völlig falsch verwendet ist
1–2 cr.: Text ist über weite Strecken unverständlich, falsche oder deutsche Wörter werden verwendet, Grammatik wird (fast) durchgehend falsch verwendet

Example
In the USA it is usual that 4-year-old girls dress up like supermodels to take part in beauty pageants. In Germany this is not very common at this young age, but many girls dream of becoming models or superstars, too. But is this really good for children? Should girls only be allowed to take part in beauty shows when they are 14 or older?
When they are really small, children don't understand what is happening around them. If girls of ten or eleven years take part in beauty pageants or shows like this, they often don't know that photos will be taken which then will be published. And later they might regret this, but they can't prevent anybody from seeing the photos anymore.
Moreover, the girls are too young to understand that sometimes they are exploited at these shows. They must "work" for hours and they don't have any time to play or spend time with their friends. So if they are allowed to take part in these shows and their parents support them, who then should tell them that this might have bad consequences?
Therefore I think that young girls under 14 shouldn't be allowed to take part in shows or beauty pageants. They can do so when they are older.

## Theme 6: Philadelphia

### Seite 94

#### 1 Finding words
1. recently – 2. suburb – 3. yard – 4. location – 5. leisure – 6. slave

#### 2 Background knowledge: American history
1. Britain's empire – 2. didn't have a say/were not represented in the British parliament – 3. tax for tea – 4. American Indians – 5. "War of Independence"/"The Revolutionary War"

#### 3 Relative clauses
1. D: Denzel's mother works at the museum which shows the history of the African-Americans.
2. N: Yesterday Denzel went there with Tom, whom he had met at school.
3. D: They both liked the room which contained some pictures of Martin Luther King best.
4. N: Their history teacher, who is very nice, had already told them about this activist.

#### 4 The present
1. is guiding – 2. is going to visit – 3. will be – 4. will read – 5. finishes

#### 5 The best job in the world
1. didn't want to go to university right away
2. a newspaper or magazine
3. travel around
4. didn't come home
5. was lucky
6. earn more money later

#### 6 Reading comprehension: the alligator hunter
1. right – 2. wrong – 3. right – 4. wrong – 5. right – 6. wrong – 7. right

#### 7 Text production: a blog entry
Example:
December 22
Today Sinead took me to Ellis Island. What a trip! This place is what they call hell on earth – or at least it must have been at the time when thousands of immigrants passed through. Even for us, it was still frightening! So many huge halls and dark buildings! I thought I might get lost, and I was really happy that I didn't have to go there on my own ...
Right at the entrance we saw the statue of Annie Moore. I had never heard her name before, but I will never forget her. After all, she came from Ireland (like me!)

and she was only 15 years old (like me!). It must have been really hard for her to travel all the way to America with only her younger brothers as company, not knowing if she would ever meet her parents again ...
I'm really glad that I can take the plane today! And even if there are problems with my parents, at least they are there for me to help me and support me.
I think I felt quite thankful for that when we walked around that sinister place!

### 8 Job application

Example:
Dear Sir or Madam,
I am interested in applying for the job as newspaper carrier that was listed on the board in your supermarket.
I am 15 years old and I would like to work at the weekends, as I still go to school. I like working outdoors, so I wouldn't mind the rainy days. I am also a very reliable and responsible person, so I think I would be a good match for the job.
I look forward to hearing from you.
Thank you for considering me for this position.
Sincerely yours,
Karen Olson

# Lösungen zur Klassenarbeit Philadelphia – Test 1

## Seite 100

Soweit nicht anders angegeben, gib dir für jede richtig gelöste Teilaufgabe einen Punkt. Bei Lückentexten gibt es für jede richtig gefüllte Lücke einen Punkt. Bei Rechtschreibfehlern ziehe dir für jeden Fehler einen halben Punkt ab.
Beachte auch die weiteren Bewertungshinweise.

### 1 Reading comprehension: the Liberty Bell

I.
1. wrong – 2. right – 3. right – 4. right – 5. wrong – 6. wrong – 7. wrong

II.
1. freedom – 2. monuments – 3. copies – 4. the USA/America – 5. American people – 6. every day – 7. terror attacks

III.
1. close – 2. 19th century – 3. German and English as the two official languages – 4. for legal texts – 5. was only one vote – 6. make integration for the German immigrants easier

### 2 Vocabulary: finding your way through Philadelphia

1. knowledge – 2. straight on – 3. cross – 4. Turn – 5. reputation – 6. incredible – 7. pride – 8. struggle

### 3 Background knowledge: history

You had to tick off:
1. unfair taxation – 2. all thirteen colonies – 3. the Declaration of Independence in Philadelphia – 4. to win over Britain – 5. had already arrived on the continent

### 4 Grammar: relative clauses

1. N: The Liberty Bell, which can be seen in Philadelphia, is considered a symbol of freedom.
2. D: The guide who waits there for tourists can tell you many legends about it.
3. D: The tourists who visit it say it's amazing.
4. N: It is located in the Independence National Historical Park, which is also very popular with tourists.
5. N: Delaware River, which was used for the trading ships, is not too far away either.
6. D: The boat which sank on Delaware River last week had been over-crowded.

### 5 Grammar: the future

1. am going to visit – 2. will take – 3. am meeting – 4. leaves

### 6 Grammar: auxiliaries

1. couldn't/weren't able to – 2. were allowed to – 3. didn't have to – 4. weren't allowed to – 5. weren't supposed to – 6. had to – 7. weren't allowed to

### 7 Text production: a blog entry

Korrigiere deinen Text oder lasse ihn von jemandem korrigieren und verteile bis zu 10 Punkte (credits = cr.) für jeden Bereich anhand der folgenden Kriterien:
Form:
9–10 cr.: der Text ist in sinnvolle Abschnitte gegliedert, durchgehend ist ein roter Faden erkennbar, durchgehend wird die persönliche Note deutlich, der Ton ist passend
7–8 cr.: der Text in Abschnitte gegliedert, ein roter Faden ist erkennbar, die persönliche Note wird meistens deutlich
5–6 cr.: der Text beginnt zusammenhanglos mit einer Information, Absätze fehlen, meistens sind die Zusammenhänge unklar
3–4 cr.: es werden keine Absätze gebildet, eine persönliche Haltung wird kaum deutlich, unterschiedliche Informationen stehen zusammenhanglos nebeneinander
1–2 cr.: einzelne unwichtige Informationen werden zusammenhanglos wiedergegeben, eine persönliche Haltung wird nicht deutlich, der Ton ist unpassen formal
Inhalt:
9–10 cr.: die Informationen sind sinnvoll ausgewählt und mit eigenen Ideen ausgebaut, die Informationen sind korrekt und schlüssig, die eigene Haltung des Schreibers wird deutlich
7–8 cr.: unterschiedliche Aspekte sind genannt, ohne dass darauf näher eingegangen wird, die Aussagen sind weitgehend persönlich und originell, der Adressat wird meistens angesprochen
5–6 cr.: im Großen und Ganzen sind sinnvolle Informationen vorhanden, der Gedankengang ist bis auf einige Stellen klar, die Aussagen sind streckenweise oberflächlich und sehr pauschal, einzelne Wiederholungen treten auf
3–4 cr.: Informationen fehlen oder sind an einzelnen Stellen falsch, nur pauschale Behauptungen ohne interessante Ausschmückungen sind vorhanden, Informationen werden aneinandergereiht

1–2 cr.: Informationen sind falsch, Aussagen sind nur pauschal und oberflächlich, Wiederholungen treten auf, Gedankengang ist wirr
Sprache:
9–10 cr.: sprachlich fehlerfrei, ganz selten Rechtschreibfehler, abwechslungsreiche Formulierungen, keine Wortwiederholungen, Sätze sind mit Nebensätzen gebildet und hängen zusammen
7–8 cr.: einzelne Fehler in Wortschatz oder Grammatik (z. B. *tenses*), manchmal werden Wörter wiederholt, einzelne Sätze sind nicht verknüpft
5–6 cr.: einfache Sätze ohne Nebensätze, häufige Fehler in Wortschatz und Grammatik (v. a. *tenses*, Satzbau), nur ganz selten sind Sätze verknüpft
3–4 cr.: an einzelnen Stellen ist der Text unverständlich, weil falsche oder deutsche Wörter verwendet werden oder die Grammatik völlig falsch verwendet ist
1–2 cr.: Text ist über weite Strecken unverständlich, falsche oder deutsche Wörter werden verwendet, Grammatik wird (fast) durchgehend falsch verwendet

Example
May 14
When I left home to go to school today I thought that today would be just another boring day. But then... We talked about the American Civil Rights movement. I can't imagine what it must be like to be forced to sit on special seats on the bus, or not to be allowed to go to the school I would like to go to!
And I think Rosa Parks is a very fascinating person! I'd really like to meet her and ask her how much courage it took to fight for equality!
Later I met Mike in the school yard. You know, he's a nice guy, but when I told him about that story he wasn't that amazed. It's only soccer and music he's interested in! Doesn't that get boring after a while? I still think the topic is awesome. Maybe it's because I can't imagine living in a world like that. None of us has ever experienced anything like that, after all ...

## Lösungen zur Klassenarbeit The world of work – Test 2

### Seite 105

Soweit nicht anders angegeben, gib dir für jede richtig gelöste Teilaufgabe einen Punkt. Bei Lückentexten gibt es für jede richtig gefüllte Lücke einen Punkt. Bei Rechtschreibfehlern ziehe dir für jeden Fehler einen halben Punkt ab.
Beachte auch die weiteren Bewertungshinweise.

#### 1 Listening comprehension: funny jobs

1. hundreds – lost – to swim – an hour
2. TV station/TV show – telling jokes/talking to the audience – 200 – part-time
3. eating – produce/sell – not many/only a few – no special
4. a fun park – make-up – 14 – 80
5. anything – tickets – agencies – reliable

#### 2 Vocabulary: the world of work

1. salary – 2. run their own business – 3. employees – 4. factory – 5. office – 6. receive – 7. staff – 8. plastic surgeon

#### 3 Background knowledge: history

1. southern – 2. workforce – 3. plantations – 4. goods – 5. Underground

#### 4 Grammar: relative clauses

1. N: John, who had started the job only two months ago, was ill last week.
2. D: The boy who had moved to Philly two years before didn't find any letterboxes.
3. D: The girl who always wears her skates for her round couldn't come because her sister was ill.
4. N: Jenny, who is at John's school, didn't come either.
5. D: On Saturday the school which most carriers attend did a day trip to the park.
6. N: The owner of the supermarket, who is usually very patient, nearly went crazy.

#### 5 Grammar: the future

1. am going to spend – 2. will need – 3. am buying – 3. finishes

#### 6 Grammar: auxiliaries

1. were supposed to be – 2. didn't have to – 3. could – 4. were not allowed to – 5. were allowed to – 6. were not allowed to – 7. could/were allowed to

#### 7 Text production: a job application

Korrigiere deinen Text oder lasse ihn von jemandem korrigieren und verteile bis zu 10 Punkte (credits = cr.) für jeden Bereich anhand der folgenden Kriterien:
Form:
9–10 cr.: Anrede und Einleitung sind formal einwandfrei, im ersten Abschnitt wird deutlich, auf welche Anzeige sich die Bewerbung bezieht, Informationen sind sinnvoll und passend dargestellt, der Ton ist formal gelungen, der Brief endet mit den üblichen Formeln und der Unterschrift
7–8 cr.: einzelne Teile einer Bewerbung fehlen, in der Einleitung wird die Anzeige genannt, die Aussage ist aber nur undeutlich, die Darstellung des Bewerbers ist meistens überzeugend gelungen, an einzelnen Stellen ist der rote Faden nicht erkennbar
5–6 cr.: mehrere Teile einer Bewerbung fehlen, in der Einleitung wird die Anzeige undeutlich genannt, die Qualifikationen sind teils unlogisch oder zu kurz genannt, an mehreren Stellen ist der rote Faden nicht erkennbar, der Ton ist nicht immer angemessen unpersönlich gelungen
3–4 cr.: mehrere Teile der Bewerbung fehlen oder sind falsch ausgeführt, in der Einleitung fehlt der Bezug zur Stellenausschreibung, die Qualifikationen sind kaum überzeugend erklärt, Zusammenhänge fehlen oft
1–2 cr.: die Teile der Bewerbung sind nicht erkennbar, im ersten Abschnitt wird kein Bezug auf die Anzeige genommen, die Qualifikationen sind unpassend und zu wenig erklärt, kein roter Faden erkennbar, Ton ist nicht angemessen unpersönlich
Inhalt:
9–10 cr.: Informationen sind gezielt für eine Bewerbung ausgewählt, die Gründe für die Bewerbung sind klar und ausführlich erklärt, der Gedankengang ist schlüssig und nachvollziehbar

7–8 cr.: einzelne Informationen sind nicht schlüssig ausgewählt, einzelne unnötige Details sind ausgeführt, der Gedankengang ist an einzelnen Stellen unklar
5–6 cr.: im Großen und Ganzen wird Bezug auf die Stellenausschreibung genommen, die Qualifikationen sind brauchbar ausgewählt und knapp erklärt, der Gedankengang ist bis auf einige Stellen klar, einzelne Wiederholungen treten auf
3–4 cr.: der Bezug auf die Anzeige ist falsch oder fehlt ganz, die Qualifikationen sind nur ganz schwach ausgewählt und kaum erklärt, die einzelnen Punkte sind nur aneinandergereiht
1–2 cr.: der Bezug zur Anzeige ist falsch wiedergegeben, die Qualifikationen sind nicht sinnvoll ausgewählt und nicht weiter erklärt, Wiederholungen treten auf, der Gedankengang ist wirr
Sprache:
9–10 cr.: sprachlich fehlerfrei, ganz selten Rechtschreibfehler, abwechslungsreiche Formulierungen, keine Wortwiederholungen, Sätze sind mit Nebensätzen gebildet und hängen zusammen
7–8 cr.: einzelne Fehler in Wortschatz oder Grammatik (z. B. *tenses*), manchmal werden Wörter wiederholt, einzelne Sätze sind nicht verknüpft
5–6 cr.: einfache Sätze ohne Nebensätze, häufige Fehler in Wortschatz und Grammatik (v. a. *tenses*, Satzbau), nur ganz selten sind Sätze verknüpft
3–4 cr.: an einzelnen Stellen ist der Text unverständlich, weil falsche oder deutsche Wörter verwendet werden oder die Grammatik völlig falsch verwendet ist
1–2 cr.: Text ist über weite Strecken unverständlich, falsche oder deutsche Wörter werden verwendet, Grammatik wird (fast) durchgehend falsch verwendet

Example
Dear Mr and Mrs Burton,
I am interested in applying for the job as a helper on your farm in August. I am 17 years old and am currently a student at Rosa-Parks-Highschool, so I will have enough time in the summer holidays in August.
I have experience in working with animals, as I have a cat and a dog myself, and I don't mind working in the stables. I am already taking driving lessons, so I have some experience in driving a vehicle, too.
I believe I would be a good match for the position because I like working outdoors and I don't mind bad weather.
I look forward to hearing from you.
Thank you for considering me for this position.
Sincerely yours,
Mike Turner